F4U CORSAIR

PART 2
THROUGH F4U-7

56

in detail & scale

Bert Kinzey

squadron/signal publications

COPYRIGHT © 1998 BY DETAIL & SCALE, INC.

This book is a product of Detail & Scale, Inc., which has sole responsibility for its content and layout, except that all contributors are responsible for the security clearance and copyright release of all materials submitted. Published by Squadron/Signal Publications, 1115 Crowley Drive, Carrollton, Texas 75011.

CONTRIBUTORS AND SOURCES:

Lloyd Jones
Wayne Morris
Larry Webster
Jim Roeder
Bill Slatton
Dick Bertea
John Muszala
J. C. Bahr
Keith Liles
Walt Fink
Stan Parker

Dave Pluth
Bob Bartolacci
Nick Waters
National Archives
U. S. Navy
U. S. Marine Corps
National Museum of Naval Aviation, Pensacola, Florida
U. S. Marine Corps Museum of Aviation, Quantico, Virginia
U. S. Marine Corps Museum, El Toro, California
War Eagles Museum, Santa Teresa, New Mexico
Battleship Park, Mobile, Alabama

Detail & Scale, Inc. and the author express a special word of thanks to Hill Goodspeed of the National Museum of Aviation and Mike Starn of the U. S. Marine Corps Museum of Aviation. Their assistance and cooperation were instrumental during the research for this publication. Lloyd Jones, Wayne Morris, and Larry Webster also deserve mention and thanks for their timely efforts which were also very important and helpful.

Many photographs in this publication are credited to their contributors. Photographs with no credit indicated were taken by the author.

ISBN 1-888974-09-5

Above (front cover photograph): Both Navy and Marine F4U-4s of CVG-4 prepare for launch from the USS CORAL SEA, CVB-43, in 1952. The carrier was operating in the Mediterranean Sea with the Sixth Fleet when this photograph was taken. The Navy Corsairs are from VF-43, while the Marine F4U-4s are assigned to VMA-201. Note the interesting tail markings on the aircraft from both units. (Syrkin NMNA)

Right (rear cover photograph): Colors and details of the instrument panel in the first XF4U-4 are revealed in this large photograph. For additional pictures of the cockpit in this Corsair, see pages 42 and 43. (Webster)

INTRODUCTION

Originally designed as a high speed fighter aircraft, the final evolution of the Corsair is exemplified in this front view of an AU-1. Each successive version of the Corsair had more ground attack capabilities than the one before it. By the time the F4U-1C and F4U-1D were produced, it had become an excellent fighter-bomber. With the AU-1, it was a dedicated close air support and attack aircraft. Its capabilities in this role are symbolized by the thirteen stations under its wings and fuselage. These include ten pylons under the outer wing panels, two pylons under the center wing section, and a centerline station. (NMNA)

This volume in the Detail & Scale Series completes our two-part coverage of Vought's famous F4U Corsair. The F4U Corsair in Detail & Scale, Part 1, covered the XF4U-1 prototype through the F2G. All production versions from the F4U-1 through the F4U-1D were included. This Part 2 contains information, general and detailed photographs, and drawings for all of the remaining Corsair variants from the F4U-4 through the F4U-7.

As the role of the Corsair evolved from fighter to fighter-bomber and finally to attack aircraft, many important changes and improvements were made to the airframe, although the proven basic design remained the same. These changes are profusely illustrated in this publication through the use of numerous close-up photographs and drawings.

To insure the highest degree of accuracy, hundreds of Vought production and delivery photographs were reviewed for selection and inclusion in this publication. Actual photographs of cockpits, engines, armament loadings, and even camera bays, taken shortly after the planes rolled off the assembly line, are included. Most of these have never been published before.

But many other features, like the redesigned elevator trim tabs on the F4U-5 or the canvas panels inside the main landing gear wells, had to be photographed on existing aircraft, because no factory photos of these items were available. To fill in the missing photos, and to pro-

vide the detailed pictorial coverage presented in this publication, trips were made by Larry Webster, Jim Roeder, Lloyd Jones, Wayne Morris, Bill Slatton, and the author to photograph several different aircraft with accurately preserved features. These included the unique XF4U-4 at the New England Air Museum and the F4U-4s at the National Museum of Naval Aviation, the U. S. Marine Corps Aviation Museum at Quantico, Virginia, and at the War Eagles Museum at Santa Teresa, New Mexico. An F4U-5N at the Marine Corps Museum at El Toro, California, and another in private hands at Chino, California, were also extensively photographed. Finally, pictures were also taken of the F4U-7 at the Battleship Park in Mobile, Alabama. From over 1,200 photographs taken on these trips, dozens were selected to illustrate every possible detail of each of the later versions of the Corsair, both inside and out.

The multi-view 1/72nd scale drawings were created by Lloyd Jones specifically for this publication, and the major changes from one version to the next are indicated. Other drawings, taken from official Navy manuals, further illustrate the details and features of the different versions of the Corsair that are covered in this book.

The National Museum of Naval Aviation and Larry Webster provided access to over a dozen official Navy manuals so that original research could be done to determine exactly what changes had been made on each version, to confirm the exact length of each variant, and to verify how many of each type were produced. This was necessary, because a considerable amount of conflicting information on these points has been published previously.

The last few pages of the book contain our usual Modelers Section which reviews the available kits of the later Corsair variants that are included in this publication. This should prove particularly helpful, because several kits have incorrect features or the wrong fuselage length. Such problems are pointed out so that they can be corrected.

HISTORICAL SUMMARY

Armed with eight five-inch rockets, this F4U-4 looks very much like its predecessor, the F4U-1D, in flight. But the characteristic chin scoop on the cowling and the exhausts above the wing help identify it as an F4U-4. Also note that this aircraft has the later windscreen design with the flat front glass. (U. S. Navy via Jones)

During its fifth test flight, which took place on May 20, 1940, the sole XF4U-1 prototype crashed landed and flipped over on a golf course in Norwich, Connecticut. Had the crash been much more severe, or had the Corsair's airframe not been so rugged, this event could have ended the development and production of two of aviation history's most successful fighter designs. Not only would the Corsair program have ended, the P-47 Thunderbolt might never have been built as well.

At that time, the U. S. Army Air Corps had decided that all of its future fighters would be powered by inline engines that afforded a more sleek aerodynamic design. But after the XF4U-1, with its huge Pratt & Whitney R-2800 radial engine, was rebuilt, it became the first fighter to exceed 400 miles-per-hour in level flight. This could hardly be ignored by the Army, and the event was instrumental in the development of the P-47 which used the same R-2800 powerplant. The irony of this is that the Corsair would remain in production until 1953, and more P-47 Thunderbolts would be built than any other American fighter in history. Yet both aircraft came so close to never being produced at all.

But as the first production F4U-1s entered service, there were still more problems to overcome and success was not immediate. The Corsair had been designed as a carrier-based fighter, but initial carrier qualifications had revealed a number of problems that were severe enough that the Navy restricted the aircraft from carrier operations until they could be solved. The port wing tended to stall before the right when flying a carrier approach, and the stiff landing gear caused a bounce that often flipped the plane over the barriers on the flight deck.

As a result, the Corsair was initially assigned to land based Marine and Navy squadrons, although the British modified landing procedures enough to begin using their Corsairs on carriers right away. Marine and Navy fighter squadrons, that replaced their older F4F Wildcats with the faster and more powerful Corsairs, were more than happy to get them. The desperate situation in the islands of the southwest Pacific demanded a fighter that could meet the Japanese on better terms.

By early 1943, Corsairs were being received by the eager pilots in squadrons that were being shipped to the Pacific theater. At Guadalcanal and elsewhere, these pilots began to achieve huge successes. VF-17 became the most successful Navy fighter squadron of all time. Marine squadrons, like "Pappy" Boyington's Black Sheep of VMF-214, became legends. In the hands of these Navy and Marine pilots, the Corsair racked up an impressive 11.3 to 1 air-to-air kill ratio. While this was considerably less than the 19 to 1 ratio achieved by the F6F Hellcat, it still remains one of the best ratios ever achieved by an American fighter. Clearly, the Corsair excelled in its intended mission as an air-to-air fighter. (Note: The Hellcat's ratio is the highest achieved by an American fighter aircraft in World War II. See the F6F Hellcat in Detail & Scale, Revised Edition, D & S Volume 49.)

But as the war progressed, the Corsair's capabilities as a fighter-bomber were continually improved. With the F4U-1A, a centerline bomb rack was fitted that could carry a single bomb weighing up to 1,000 pounds. Two additional pylons were added under the center wing section on the F4U-1C and F4U-1D. During production of these two variants, the capability to carry eight 5-inch rockets under the outer wing sections was also added.

The change in role from fighter to fighter-bomber happened for two reasons. First, there was a need for more aircraft to attack the enemy on the ground, and the

F4U-1A, BuNo. 49763, was one of two F4U-1As converted to XF4U-4X prototypes. Note the older canopy with the two overhead frames. The other XF4U-4X was converted from F4U-1A, BuNo. 50301. These two aircraft should not be confused with the five XF4U-4 prototypes which were BuNos. 80759 through 80763.

(U. S. Navy via Jones)

large powerful Corsair had the capability for being a very successful fighter-bomber. Second, as the war continued, there was less and less air opposition from the Japanese. So the tactical situation dictated that the Corsair, as well as other fighters, would be increasingly used to attack targets on the ground rather than those in the air. While the Corsair continued to be a very successful air-to-air fighter throughout World War II, an increasingly greater percentage of missions were flown against ground targets during the final year of the war.

By the second half of 1944, the problems associated with carrier landings had been solved, and Corsairs were being assigned to fleet carriers in ever increasing numbers. Both the F6F Hellcat and the F4U Corsair were so successful at attacking surface targets with bombs and rockets, the Navy began increasing the ratio of fighters to torpedo and dive bombers in their air wings. By war's end, the majority of aircraft in the air wings assigned to fleet carriers were fighters, and the number of bomber types continued to dwindle. It was said that once a Corsair or a Hellcat delivered its bombs and rockets, it could still serve effectively as a fighter for the rest of the mission. But once an Avenger or a Helldiver delivered its ordnance, it was nothing more than a target. While there were missions best performed by the larger Avengers and Helldivers, it is understandable why the Navy wanted to have as many fighters aboard its carriers as possible. For a more extensive account of the Corsair's service in World War II, and for a detailed look at the earlier variants, see

The F4U Corsair in Detail & Scale, Part 1, D&S Volume 55.

The final Corsair variant to see action in World War II was the F4U-4. It was powered by an R-2800-18W engine, although the R-2800-42W was later installed. The F4U-4 also had a completely redesigned cockpit interior which had a floor and full consoles on each side. In today's terminology, the cockpit design was more ergonomic than that found in the floorless cockpits of the "dash 1" Corsairs. Otherwise, the F4U-4 was essentially the same as the F4U-1D. F4U-4s reached the combat areas during the final months of World War II, and they served with both Navy and Marine squadrons. One was flown by Marine Captain John Glenn, who later became an astronaut and a United States Senator from Ohio.

In September 1945 the war ended, and the United States cancelled many military contracts. Those that survived were slashed. Brewster had failed the year before, and was no longer involved in the production Corsairs, but Goodyear had just begun producing their equivalent of the F4U-4 which was designated the FG-4. Production was halted, and the dozen or so aircraft that had been completed by Goodyear were scrapped. Vought was allowed to proceed with the F4U-4, but the number of aircraft on order was significantly reduced. A total of 2,356 were produced, and this included 140 cannon armed F4U-4Bs and 11 F4U-4P photographic reconnaissance aircraft.

In the years immediately following World War II, the development of jet engines continued at a fast pace, and this meant that the days of propeller-driven fighters were coming to a close. But the Navy wisely realized that for some time to come, aircraft with piston engines would remain very effective for ground attack work. Development began on several propeller-driven attack types, the most successful of which would ultimately result in the Douglas A-1 Skyraider. But the success of the Corsair in this role during World War II meant that the Navy and

Marine Corsairs often operated aboard the Navy's escort carriers. Here, F4U-4s from VMA-332 prepare for launch from the USS POINT CRUZ, CVE-119, in November 1953. (NMNA)

This Marine F4U-4 from VMF-235, is lowered to the hangar bay on one of the elevators on the USS CAPE ESPERANCE, CVE-88. (NMNA)

Marines already had a viable attack and ground support aircraft on hand. Clearly, the capability of the Corsair to serve in ground attack roles is what allowed it to remain in production until 1953 and in service for several years thereafter.

The first Corsair variant to be developed and produced in the post-war years was the F4U-5. The changes and improvements on this version were more radical and significant than between any two successive variants that had come before. A much more powerful engine was installed, and the forward fuselage was both lengthened and widened as a result. Machine gun armament was deleted once and for all, and four 20-mm cannons became the standard for this and all subsequent Corsair variants. Cowl flaps, the oil cooler doors, and the intercooler dump flap were all automatically controlled. The trim tabs were electrically operated. The fabric covering on the wings was replaced with a metal skin, and this reduced drag considerably. The canopy was changed to a blown design that afforded better visibility, particularly to the rear.

When the "dash 5" series of Corsairs were produced, there was still some belief and intention that they would serve in the conventional air-to-air role to some extent. In

fact, most of the Corsairs in the "dash 5" series were F4U-5N and F4U-5NL night fighters, and while they would be used to some degree in this role during the Korean War, even these would actually fly more missions attacking targets on the ground along with standard F4U-4, F4U-4B, and F4U-5 fighter-bombers. Thirty F4U-5P photo reconnaissance Corsairs were also produced.

When the Korean War began, the Corsair was the most numerous fighter-bomber in the Navy, Naval Reserve, and Marine inventories. The Douglas Skyraider, a superb attack aircraft, was also in service, but the Corsair was available in larger numbers and ready to do the work that was required. Within a few days after the communists invaded, Corsairs were flying missions from aircraft carriers lying off the Korean coast. Corsairs operated from Japan, and they were also deployed to bases on the Korean peninsula. They would continue to serve in combat until the hostilities ceased in July 1953.

This is not to say that jet fighters, like the F9F Panther and F2H Banshee in the Navy and Marine Corps, and the F-80 Shooting Star and F-84 Thunderjet in the U. S. Air Force, did not fly many missions against ground targets during the Korean War. But it was clear to all ser-

Although it appeared to be very similar to the previous F4U-4, the F4U-5 was quite different from its predecessor. The fuselage was longer and wider due to a larger powerplant, and the forward fuselage was completely redesigned. The F4U-5 was also the first Corsair variant to have wings that were completely covered with a metal skin. This F4U-5 was assigned to VMF-224 and photographed at MCAS, Cherry Point, North Carolina, in 1948. (NMNA)

Most "dash 5" Corsairs were completed as F4U-5N or F4U-5NL night fighters. These could be distinguished by the radar pod on the leading edge of the right wing. This F4U-5N was assigned to the Flying Nightmares of VMF(N)-513, and it was photographed in November 1950. (NMNA)

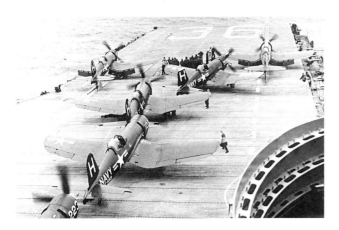

Navy F4U-4s from VF-653 are launched from the USS ANTETIAM, CV-36. *(NMNA)*

During the Korean War, Corsairs operated from fields throughout Korea as they provided close air support to UN forces on the ground. These rocket armed F4U-4Bs were assigned to VMF-323. *(NMNA)*

vices that propeller-driven aircraft could fly many of these missions more effectively than these first generation jet fighters.

As a result, the Air Force called on the F-51D Mustangs it still had in service, and although they performed well in Korea, the inline, liquid-cooled engines were very vulnerable to ground fire. As a result, loss rates for the F-51Ds were extremely high. Many Mustang pilots in Korea, who had flown the P-47 in World War II, openly stated their preference for the Thunderbolt and its large air-cooled radial engine which was far less susceptible to ground fire. But that engine was precisely what was in the Corsair, and accordingly, it suffered a much lower loss rate than the Mustang in Korea. Corsairs also had another advantage over the Mustangs in Korea in that they could carry a heavier ordnance load.

Lt. Guy Bordelon became the Navy's only ace during the Korean War, and he did so flying F4U-5Ns at night. Marine Captain Jesse Folmar shot down a MiG-15 while flying an F4U-4B. Another reference has stated that this was the first time a propeller-driven fighter had destroyed

a jet fighter in flight, but this is not the case. A number of Me 262 jet fighters were shot down by propeller-driven fighters during World War II, but Folmar's accomplishment was still noteworthy considering the considerable speed advantage of his adversary.

In spite of the relatively few air-to-air encounters experienced by Corsair pilots during the Korean War, the overwhelming majority of missions were flown against ground targets. The days when the Corsair would rack up impressive kill ratios over enemy aircraft were now only a part of history, yet its service in another role was just as significant and valuable in a different war in a different place at a later time.

After becoming a legendary squadron during World War II, the Black Sheep of VMF-214 went back to war again in Korea. Here, an F4U-4B gets the signal to launch from an escort carrier for a mission against the communists. Note the two radio altimeter antennas under the aft fuselage. *(U. S. Navy via Jones)*

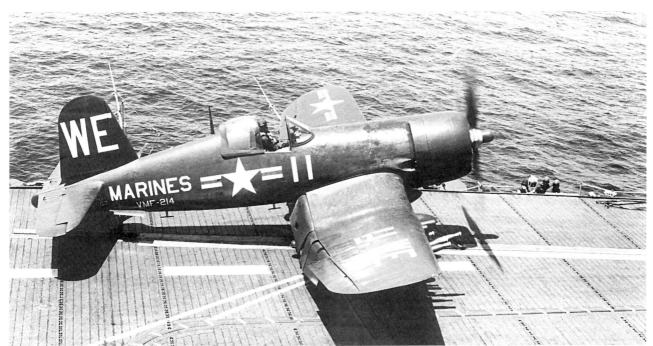

The AU-1 was a dedicated ground attack version of the Corsair, and it was the last variant to be built for U. S. service. This AU-1 was assigned to VMA-323, and it is loaded with ordnance for a mission against communist targets in Korea. **(NMNA)**

The final variant produced for U. S. forces exemplifies the end of the progression from air superiority fighter to attack aircraft that the Corsair experienced over its operational service. Originally called the XF4U-6, the designation was changed to AU-1 to indicate the dedicated ground attack role for the aircraft. Fitted with additional armor plating to protect its undersides from ground fire, and equipped with an engine optimized for low level operations, there was no longer any pretense that this Corsair was a fighter in the contemporary sense of the word. Extra hardpoints were added under its wings so that every ounce of ordnance the aircraft was capable of lifting could be delivered to the enemy. The production of 111 AU-1s was completed in 1952, and many were used by the Marines during the second half of the Korean War. After the war, they remained in service with both the Navy and Marines, and they were among the last Corsairs to be retired from U. S. service.

The Lancers of VMA-212 flew AU-1s in Korea. Several of their aircraft are shown here loaded with fragmentation bombs and ready for another mission. **(NMNA)**

AU-1, BuNo. 129378, was based at MCAS, Quantico, Virginia, and it was one of the last three Corsairs in service with the U. S. Marine Corps. **(NMNA)**

The last version of the Corsair to be produced was the F4U-7, ninety-four of which were built for the French Navy. **(NMNA)**

The final ninety-four Corsairs to roll off the assembly line were produced exclusively for the French Navy (Aeronavale). These were supplied under the Military Assistance Program (MAP), and deliveries were made in the second half of 1952 and early 1953. On January 31, 1953, F4U-7, BuNo. 133832, became the last Corsair to be completed, thus ending production almost thirteen years after the crash of the XF4U-1 prototype which almost ended the program before it began.

After being phased out of service with the U. S. Navy and Marines, F4U-7s and a few AU-1s remained opera-

tional with the French until 1964. Several F4U-4s, F4U-5Ns, and F4U-5NLs were acquired by Honduras, and Argentina received twenty-six F4U-5, F4U-5N, and F4U-5NL Corsairs. In 1969, Corsairs flown by El Salvador and Honduras engaged each other in aerial combat, and the last aerial victory scored by a Corsair was against another Corsair. This marked an interesting end to the military service of the aircraft. El Salvador flew the last known Corsair mission by a foreign nation in 1971.

For many years after their military service, Corsairs were among the most popular racing planes acquired by wealthy civilians. Some were little changed from their military configurations except for the often colorful and elaborate paint schemes that were usually applied to them. Others received significant physical modifications to lessen weight, enhance streamlining, and improve speed and performance in unlimited air racing. Most popular of these were the powerful F2Gs that had been built before that variant was cancelled after only a handful had been completed.

Today, almost ninety Corsairs still exist. A few are not much more than hulks that are being rebuilt. Some are very accurately restored in museums, and still others are privately owned and flown at air shows and demonstrations. While the majority of remaining Corsairs are later aircraft that were built after World War II, aviation enthusiasts can rejoice in the knowledge that a few World War II Corsairs still exist and are being preserved for future generations.

Honduras, El Salvador, and Argentina all flew Corsairs after the Korean War. These F4U-4s still have their Honduran medium blue and white markings after being returned to the United States following their service in South America. **(NMNA)**

CORSAIR VARIANTS
F4U-4 & F4U-4B

F4U-4Bs were the cannon-armed equivalents of the F4U-4. On this sub-variant, and the cannon-armed "dash 5" Corsairs that followed, the rockets were carried on stub pylons beneath the outer wing panels. These pylons were mounted in a staggered arrangement, with one being located on the leading edge of the wing directly below the outboard cannon. (NMNA)

There were two major changes that differentiated the F4U-4 from the F4U-1D which immediately preceded it. First, the engine was changed to the R-2800-18W "C" series powerplant. This was later replaced with the R-2800-42W during the F4U-4 production run. Second, the cockpit interior was completely redesigned. These two changes also differentiated the cannon armed F4U-4B from the previous F4U-1C. The F4U-4 and the F4U-4B differed only in that the F4U-4 was armed with six .50-caliber Browning machine guns with 2,400 rounds of ammunition, while the F4U-4B had four M-3 20-mm cannon with 924 rounds of ammunition.

The new powerplant resulted in five physical changes to the forward and lower fuselage. First, the three-blade propeller, used on all production Corsairs prior to the "dash 4" series, was replaced with a Hamilton-Standard four-blade propeller. Second, the engine itself had a larger cylindrical crankcase with numerous bolts holding the assembly together. Third, the increased air require-

ments for the more powerful engine necessitated the addition of a scoop at the bottom of the cowl ring. Fourth, the exhausts were redesigned. Instead of having three stubs located together on each side of the cowling, two stubs were moved to a position above the level of the wing on each side of the forward fuselage. Only one stub remained below the wing level on each side. Finally, the vent door for the engine accessory compartment and intercoolers was completely redesigned. This door was located just aft of the cowling on the underside of the aircraft.

The layout of the cockpit was completely redesigned. All previous Corsair variants had a floorless cockpit with two foot troughs below the rudder pedals. Beginning with the F4U-4 and F4U-4B, a floor was added, and items on the sides of the cockpit were rearranged on side consoles. A center console was added below the main instrument panel, and it extended to the floor between the rudder pedals. The conventional seat was replaced with a seat bucket, while the back of the seat was formed by armor plate that was attached to the rear bulkhead.

A common misconception about another feature on the F4U-4 has to do with the windscreen. Most other references on the Corsair have stated that the F4U-4 had a flat windscreen instead of the rounded one used on the F4U-1A, -C, and -D. While this flat bulletproof windscreen did appear during the production of the F4U-4,

This F4U-4 from VMF-225 was photographed in 1946, and it shows some unusual markings used by the Marines shortly after World War II. **(NMNA)**

almost half of the F4U-4s had the earlier rounded windscreen. The five prototypes, BuNos. 80759 through 80763, and the first 995 production F4U-4s, BuNos. 80764 through 81758, had the rounded windscreen. The following twenty aircraft off the production line, BuNos. 81759 through 81778, had the flat bulletproof windscreen. These were followed by fifty more F4U-4s, BuNos. 81779 through 81828, which had the rounded windscreen. BuNo. 81829 and subsequent had the flat windscreen design. Therefore, out of the 2,356 F4U-4s, F4U-4Bs, and -4Ps produced, 1,045, or just over forty-four percent, had the original round windscreen.

The capability to carry external stores was essentially the same as it had been for the F4U-1C and -1D. But the two pylons under the center wing section were redesigned and strengthened so that they could each carry an 11.75-inch "Tiny Tim" rocket. During the operational service of the F4U-4, pylons or rails were designed that could be attached to the outer wing panels in place of the zero-length rocket stubs. Bomb racks could then be fitted to these rails, and small 100 or 250-pound bombs could be loaded to these racks. These were often used in Korea when bombs were better choices than rockets for the particular targets being attacked.

On the F4U-4B, the use of cannon armament resulted in a different hardpoint arrangement under the outer wing panels. Four stub pylons were mounted in a staggered arrangement under each wing, and one of the pylons was

With a 150-gallon fuel tank on the right pylon under the center wing section, an F4U-4 taxis forward after landing aboard the USS TARAWA, CV-40, on September 5, 1951. **(NMNA)**

Rocket armed F4U-4Bs from VMF-323 operated from primitive field conditions in Korea during August 1951. Note the overspray of white paint on the tail of the aircraft in the foreground. **(NMNA)**

With four 5-inch rockets loaded on its staggered stub pylons, an F4U-4B makes a deck run to launch from an escort carrier. The stub pylon, mounted on the leading edge directly under the outboard cannon, is easy to see on the right wing of this Corsair. (U. S. Navy via Jones)

located on the leading edge of the wing directly under the muzzle of the outer cannon. This arrangement of stub pylons would also be used on the "dash 5" series of Corsairs as well.

Several different numbers have been published concerning the quantity of F4U-4Bs produced. These numbers range as high as 297. However, Navy records indicate that only 140 were built. These were BuNos. 97391 through 97531. Of the other 2,216 aircraft in the "dash 4" production run, one was completed as an XF4U-4N night fighter prototype which led to the development of

the F4U-5N and F4U-5NL. Five were classified as XF4U-4s, three became XF4U-5 prototypes, and eleven were completed as F4U-4P photo reconnaissance aircraft. The remaining 2,196 were built as standard F4U-4 fighters.

Numbers also vary between nine and twelve when it comes to the quantity of F4U-4Ps produced, but Navy records indicate that eleven examples of this sub-variant were built. They have often been confused, particularly when it comes to service in Korea, with the later F4U-5P, of which thirty were produced. The eleven F4U-4Ps retained the armament of the standard F4U-4, but they had a camera installed in the aft fuselage. Photographs could be taken through windows in the bottom and the left side of the fuselage. There was no window on the right side as there was on the later F4U-5P. F4U-4Ps also did not have the fairing on the vertical tail which was characteristic of the F4U-5P. For detailed photographs of the F4U-4P, see pages 24 and 25.

Small general purpose or fragmentary bombs could also be loaded on the stub pylons of the F4U-4B. This Corsair is from VMF-312, and it was photographed in Korea during late 1951. (NMNA)

F4U-4 DETAILS
WINDSCREEN & CANOPY

Above: A common misconception about the F4U-4 is that it had a flat windscreen. While this feature was added about mid-way through the production run, 1,045 F4U-4s, including the five XF4U-4 prototypes, had this rounded windscreen. These included BuNos. 80764 through 81758, and 81779 through 81828. This photo was taken of the windscreen on the first XF4U-4 prototype, BuNo. 80759. (Webster)

Above right: F4U-4s, BuNos. 81759 through 81778, and 81829 and subsequent had the flat windscreen as illustrated in this photograph. Note how close together the two forward frames are at the top of the windscreen. (Vought)

Right: The canopy remained basically the same as it had before, but it was flattened slightly at the top in order to fit the new windscreen. (Vought)

On the earlier canopy, as used with the rounded windscreen, there was a "U"-shaped extention on the aft frame above and behind the pilot's head. It was deleted from the canopy that was used with the flat windscreen.

Note how the forward end of the canopy rides above the side of the fuselage when open. The rear of the canopy had a roller that moved along a rail in the side of the fuselage.

COCKPIT DETAILS

The cockpit of the F4U-4 was quite different than the ones in previous Corsair variants. Most notably, there was a floor instead of the open fuselage with foot troughs below the rudder pedals. A center console was added beneath the instrument panel, and it extended down to the floor between the rudder pedals. (Vought)

The instrument panel in the F4U-4B was essentially identical to that in the F4U-4. The detail differences were related to the different armament of four 20-mm cannons instead of six .50-caliber machine guns. Master armament switches for the guns were located on the eyebrow panel to the left of the gun sight, so there are only four switches in this F4U-4B cockpit as compared to six in the photograph of the F4U-4's instrument panel at left. Rocket and bomb switches were on the right eyebrow panel. (Vought)

Full consoles were installed in the F4U-4 and F4U-4B, and the items on each side of the cockpit were arranged in a more logical and easily accessible manner than in the "dash 1" Corsairs. This is the left console with the throttle quadrant and trim wheels. The landing gear was controlled by a lever on the auxiliary panel at the forward end of the console. The side consoles were the same in the F4U-4 and F4U-4B. (Vought)

The console on the right side of the cockpit is shown here. Circuit breakers were on the vertical side of the console forward of the seat. The slanted forward portion of the console had electrical controls, the engine primer, and starter switch. The horizontal area was the radio control panel. The coiled cord was for the hand microphone. (Vought)

ENGINE DETAILS

Above: Several features that first appeared on the F4U-4 are illustrated in this photograph. These include the Hamilton-Standard four-blade propeller, the larger cylindrical crankcase of the R-2800-18W engine with the dozens of bolts holding it together, and the air scoop at the bottom of the cowling. (Vought)

Above right: Initially, the F4U-4 had the R-2800-18W powerplant installed. Later, this was changed to the more powerful R-2800-42W, which was similar in appearance. This is the left side of an engine assembly which is ready for installation in the aircraft. (Vought)

Center right: Details on the right side of the engine assembly are illustrated here. (Vought)

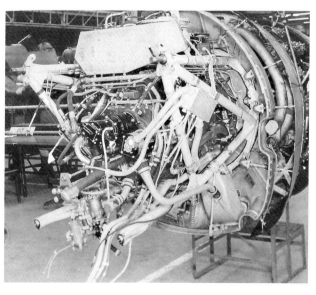

Right: The engine accessories were located inside the mounting frame, and they were surrounded by numerous tubes and wires. Note the locations of the three exhausts on this side of the engine assembly. (Vought)

EXHAUST DETAILS

On all production versions up through the F4U-1D, the three exhaust stubs on each side were located together below the level of the wing. On the F4U-4, only one stub remained in this location as can be seen here. The other two stubs were moved to a position above the level of the wing. The ends of the stubs are visible in this photo, and they can be seen protruding just aft of the open cowl flaps.

Indented areas in the forward fuselage provided clearance for the exhausts on each side. These are the two for the exhausts on the left side.

This view looks forward over the top of the wing, and it shows the two exhaust stubs above the wing on the right side of the aircraft.

An underside view provides a look at the two lower exhausts and their single stubs. The upper exhaust on the left side can also be seen above the level of the wing. Also note that the cowl flaps do not go all the way around the bottom of the cowling. Instead, they end just about even with the lower exhaust stubs.

UNDERSIDE DETAILS

The vent door for the engine accessory compartment and intercooler was completely redesigned for the more powerful engine installed in the F4U-4.

This close-up provides a look at the open vent door for the right oil cooler intake.

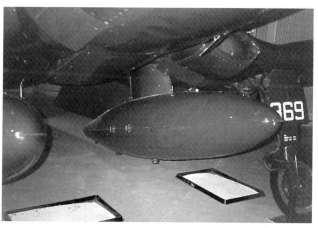

The two pylons under the center wing section of this F4U-4 have 150-gallon fuel tanks attached to them. The partially open vent door for the engine accessory compartment and intercooler is visible between the two pylons.

The same area shown at left is seen here again from the other side. Note the details of the intake in the left wing root. Silver placards on the side of the tank provide information about fueling and attaching the tank to the pylon.

This close-up of the left pylon under the center wing section also shows the open vent door for the left intake.

In this view, the pylon is covered with its protective fairing, and the tank is on a dolly below it. Note the fitting on the tank where it joins the pylon.   (Slatton)

LANDING GEAR DETAILS

A close-up reveals the details on the inside of the left main landing gear wheel.   (Slatton)

A closer view provides a look at the retraction cylinder and the forward part of the gear well.   (Slatton)

Details at the front end of the left main wheel well are illustrated here. The cylinders which actuated the doors are clearly visible, as is the top of the retraction cylinder for the main gear strut.   (Webster)

The outer gear door and outside of the left gear well are shown here.   (Webster)

A canvas cover fit over an oval shaped panel on the inner wall of the gear well. The cover is shown here in the open position. Also note the shape of the inner door for the left gear well.   (Webster)

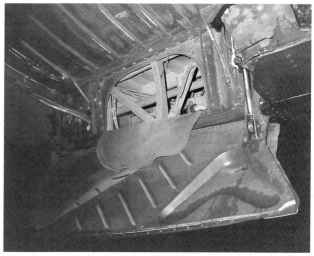

The inside wall of the left main gear well also had an oval shaped panel with a canvas cover. Again, the cover has been opened to reveal the structure behind it. (Webster)

An overall view of the right main gear provides a look at the outside of the wheel and the strut. The struts and wheels were usually a steel color on later Corsairs, but in some cases, they were painted the same color as the underside of the wing. This usually happened when the aircraft was repainted at a field repair and maintenance facility. (Webster)

A view of the aft end of the left main gear well illustrates that it was almost devoid of any features. (Webster)

The tail gear is shown here in the retracted position. Note the fairings on the tail wheel doors just aft of the opening for the wheel.

Both the tail gear and the arresting hook are shown here from the left side. The wheel has castored around ninety degrees as the aircraft was pushed back to this position.

WING DETAILS

Vanes located inside the air intakes in each wing root routed air to the intercooler located inside the fuselage. Oil coolers were located at the outer end of each intake.

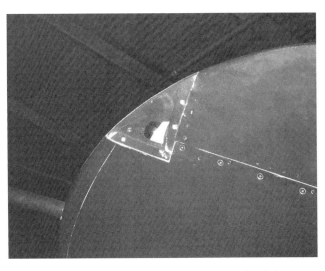

The navigation lights on the wing tips remained the same for all Corsair variants. This is the red light on the left wing. The red bulb is located under a clear cover.

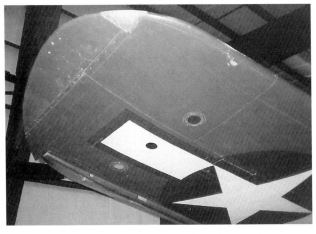

The F4U-4/-4B was the last Corsair variant to have three identification lights under the right wing tip. They were red, blue, and amber from front to rear. This feature was deleted on the F4U-5. (Webster)

These pylons could be bolted to the outer wing panels in place of the zero-length rocket launchers often seen in this location. Bomb racks could be attached to these pylons, and small general purpose or fragmentary bombs could be carried on them.

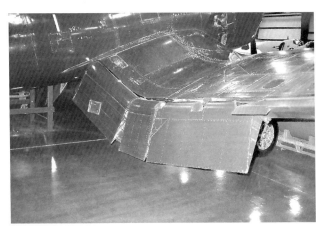

The design of the three-section flaps on each wing remained as it had been on the F4U-1D. The F4U-4 and F4U-4B had the step cutout in the inboard right flap, however on this aircraft it is covered with a clear plastic plate. (Webster)

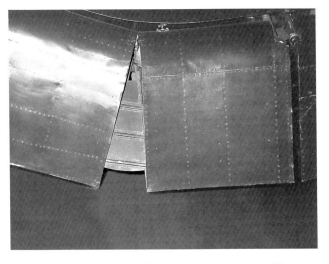

As with all other Corsairs, a spanner or gap filler was present between the inboard and center flaps on each wing. (Webster)

TAIL DETAILS

On most Corsairs up through the F4U-1D, antenna wires had usually been attached to a stub mast at the top of the rudder. On the F4U-4/-4B, the wires were most often attached to the top of the vertical stabilizer as shown here.

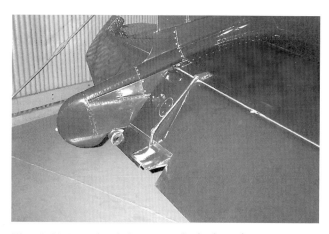

The F4U-4 retained the same dual trim tab arrangement on each elevator as had been used on all "dash 1" Corsairs.

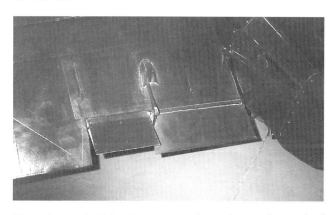

The tabs on the left elevator are shown here. A standard trim tab was inboard on each elevator, and a smaller balance tab was mounted outboard. The balance tab was controlled by an actuator that entered the elevator as seen in this view.

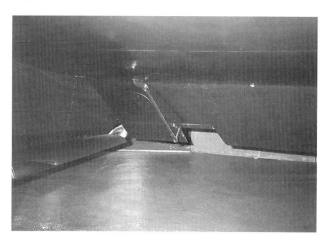

The trim tab had a longer actuating arm that entered the trailing edge of the horizontal stabilizer on the opposite side from the actuator for the balance tab. Since the two horizontal tail assemblies were interchangeable, the actuators on the right elevator were the reverse of what is shown here. Accordingly, the longer arm for the trim tab was on the upper surface of the right elevator as shown in the top right photograph above.

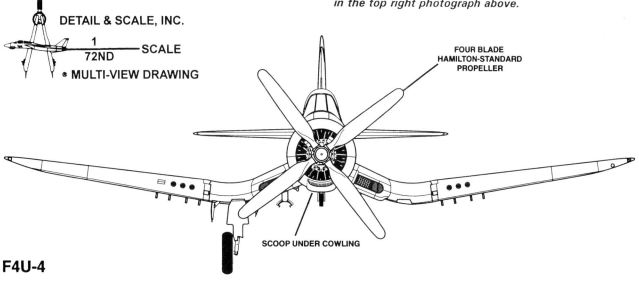

DETAIL & SCALE, INC.

$\frac{1}{72ND}$ SCALE

® MULTI-VIEW DRAWING

FOUR BLADE
HAMILTON-STANDARD
PROPELLER

SCOOP UNDER COWLING

F4U-4

DETAIL & SCALE COPYRIGHT © DRAWING BY LLOYD S. JONES

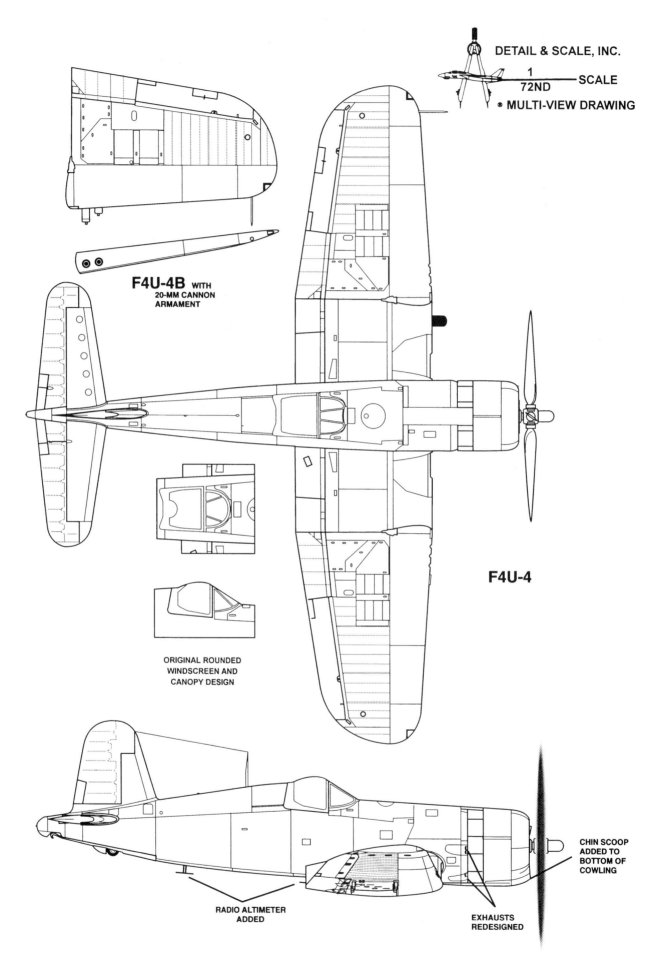

$\dfrac{1}{72ND}$ SCALE

® MULTI-VIEW DRAWING

F4U-4B WITH
20-MM CANNON
ARMAMENT

F4U-4

ORIGINAL ROUNDED
WINDSCREEN AND
CANOPY DESIGN

CHIN SCOOP
ADDED TO
BOTTOM OF
COWLING

RADIO ALTIMETER
ADDED

EXHAUSTS
REDESIGNED

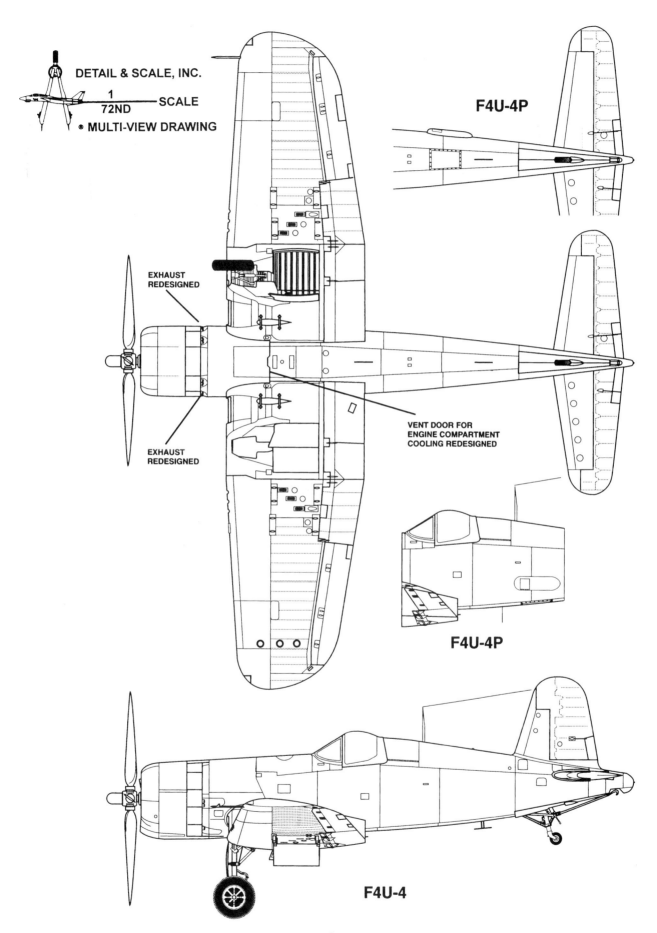

DETAIL & SCALE, INC.

$\dfrac{1}{72ND}$ ——— SCALE

® MULTI-VIEW DRAWING

F4U-4P

EXHAUST
REDESIGNED

EXHAUST
REDESIGNED

VENT DOOR FOR
ENGINE COMPARTMENT
COOLING REDESIGNED

F4U-4P

F4U-4

DETAIL & SCALE COPYRIGHT © DRAWINGS BY LLOYD S. JONES

F4U-4P

Above: Eleven F4U-4Ps were built, and they could be identified by a camera window in the bottom of the fuselage and another on the left side. In this photograph, the left side camera window can be seen inside the lower part of the star in the national insignia. These photo reconnaissance aircraft retained the full armament capability of the F4U-4 including the zero-length rocket launchers under the wings. *(Vought)*

Right: The instrument panel in the F4U-4P looked very much like that found in the standard F4U-4 except for the area at the very center of the panel. *(Vought)*

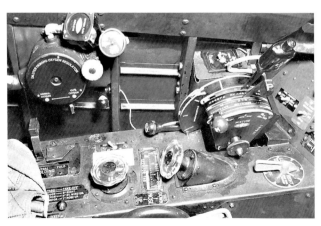

Details on the throttle quadrant and the left console are illustrated here. *(Vought)*

The right side of the cockpit in the F4U-4P had only minor detail differences from that installed in the standard fighter version. *(Vought)*

CAMERA BAY DETAILS

Access to the camera bay in the F4U-4P was through a large door on the right side of the fuselage. The interior of the bay was painted Chromate Green. *(Vought)*

With no camera installed, details in the interior of the camera bay are visible here. Both the vertical and oblique camera windows and mounts are shown. *(Vought)*

A K-17, 24-inch camera is installed in the vertical position in this view. *(Vought)*

In this photo, the same camera has been installed in the oblique position. *(Vought)*

The oblique camera window was on the left side of the fuselage. It was covered by an oval shaped blister with a sliding door. The door is shown here in the closed position. *(Vought)*

With the door open, the camera's lens is visible through the square window. *(Vought)*

F4U-5

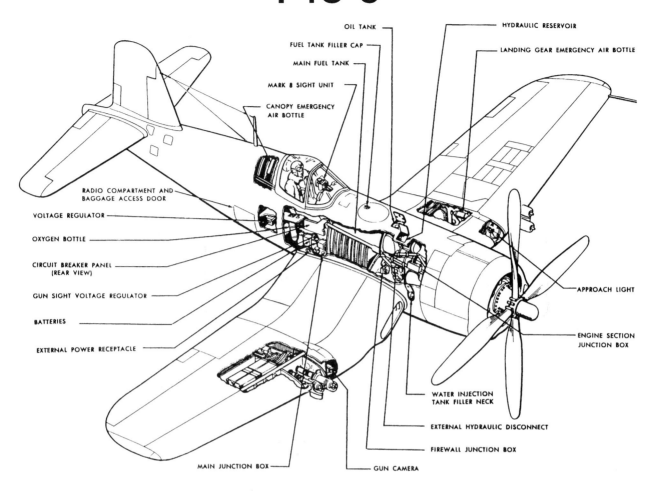

OIL TANK

FUEL TANK FILLER CAP

MAIN FUEL TANK

MARK 8 SIGHT UNIT

CANOPY EMERGENCY AIR BOTTLE

HYDRAULIC RESERVOIR

LANDING GEAR EMERGENCY AIR BOTTLE

RADIO COMPARTMENT AND BAGGAGE ACCESS DOOR

VOLTAGE REGULATOR

OXYGEN BOTTLE

CIRCUIT BREAKER PANEL (REAR VIEW)

GUN SIGHT VOLTAGE REGULATOR

BATTERIES

EXTERNAL POWER RECEPTACLE

APPROACH LIGHT

ENGINE SECTION JUNCTION BOX

WATER INJECTION TANK FILLER NECK

EXTERNAL HYDRAULIC DISCONNECT

FIREWALL JUNCTION BOX

MAIN JUNCTION BOX

GUN CAMERA

The major components of the F4U-5 are illustrated in this general arrangement drawing.   *(U. S. Navy)*

The first Corsair variant to be developed and flown after the end of World War II was the F4U-5. Although it may have looked much like the previous F4U-4 at first glance, it was a radically different aircraft in many respects. The first XF4U-5 prototype made its initial flight on April 4, 1946. The first production F4U-5 day fighter flew for the first time on May 12, 1947.

Perhaps the most noticeable difference was in the forward fuselage. The change to the R-2800-32W "E" series powerplant, with its two-stage, variable-speed supercharger, necessitated the lengthening of the nose section by approximately ten inches. There has been conflicting information concerning the fuselage lengths of later Corsair variants in other publications. Official Navy and Vought manuals give the fuselage length of the F4U-5, including the F4U-5N, F4U-5NL, and F4U-5P, as 34' 6.15". It is also the official length stated by the manuals for the AU-1. This compares to an official length of 33' 8.25" for the F4U-4, F4U-4B, and F4U-7.

The air required for the R-2800-32W also resulted in another change to the design of the cowling. Instead of the scoop at the bottom of the cowl ring, as found on the F4U-4 and F4U-4B, all Corsairs in the "dash 5" series had two cheek scoops. When viewing the cowl from the front, these scoops would be at the four and eight o'clock positions. Fairings for these scoops were noticeable on each side of the forward fuselage, and they caused the forward fuselage to be approximately eight inches wider

than on earlier Corsairs. Within the cowling, the engine was mounted with a slight downward angle to drop its thrust line by 2.75 degrees. This improved the longitudinal stability of the aircraft and increased forward visibility.

But there were other changes to the forward fuselage as well. The cooling flaps were completely redesigned, and they extended all the way across the underside of the cowling. There was a section on each side of the cowling

The identifying feature of the "dash 5" series of Corsairs was the longer and wider forward fuselage section with the cheek scoops on the lip of the cowling.   *(Vought)*

The stub pylons used under the outer wing panels on the "dash 5" Corsairs were the same as had been used on the F4U-4B. They were arranged in a staggered pattern, with one being located directly on the leading edge beneath the outboard cannon. (NMNA)

that did not have any cooling flaps. This was a completely different arrangement than on any previous Corsair variant. Operation of these cooling flaps was fully automatic. Automatic control for the oil cooler doors and intercooler dump flap was also added to the F4U-5, but a manual override was provided for each system. The exhausts were also redesigned, and the upper stubs on each side of the fuselage were located slightly higher than those on the F4U-4.

The F4U-5 was the first Corsair variant to delete fabric covering on the outer wing panels. This area was skinned with metal on the F4U-5, as well as all subsequent versions of the Corsair, and this resulted in a reduction in drag. The three identification lights, located under the right wing tip on previous Corsairs, were deleted. The single blue light, one of which had been on top of each wing near the tip on earlier versions, was relocated to the same position on the underside of each wing.

The horizontal stabilizers were fabricated from a Vought-developed substance known as Metalite, and this did away with the round access panels on the top of the left stabilizer and the bottom of the right one. The trim tabs on the elevators were also redesigned, and this eliminated the twin tab arrangement found on earlier versions. Instead of each elevator having both a trim tab and a balance tab, F4U-5s had a single large trim tab on each elevator that was electrically controlled.

Entry to the cockpit was also changed. The cut out step in the inboard right flap was deleted, and a retractable boarding step on the right side of the fuselage replaced it. Steps in the sides of the fuselage above the wing were also modified. The canopy was once again enlarged to a blown design, and it was higher than that used on the F4U-4. In order for the aft end of this new canopy to fit with the top of the fuselage, a fairing was added to the spine just aft of the cockpit. This fairing was quite noticeable whenever the canopy was in the closed position.

A few changes were also made inside the cockpit, and the most noticeable of these was the elimination of the lower part of the instrument panel that was located between the rudder pedals. Pilot comfort was emphasized, and a new heater, located in the lower fuselage, provided both cockpit heating and windshield defrosting.

A new centerline pylon was added, and a bomb up to 2,000 pounds in weight could be carried on this station. The two pylons under the center wing section remained the same as they had been on the previous F4U-4. The four stub pylons under each outer wing panel were the ones first introduced on the F4U-4B. They were mounted in the same staggered arrangement which was necessitated by the cannon armament. Internal armament was four M-3 20-mm cannon with 924 rounds of ammunition.

A total of 223 F4U-5 fighters were produced, but the most numerous "dash 5" sub-variant was the F4U-5N/-NL night fighter as described beginning on page 49. Thirty F4U-5P reconnaissance aircraft were also built, and information on these can be found on pages 30 through 32. F4U-5s served with the Navy and Marines, and a few were provided to Argentina and Honduras.

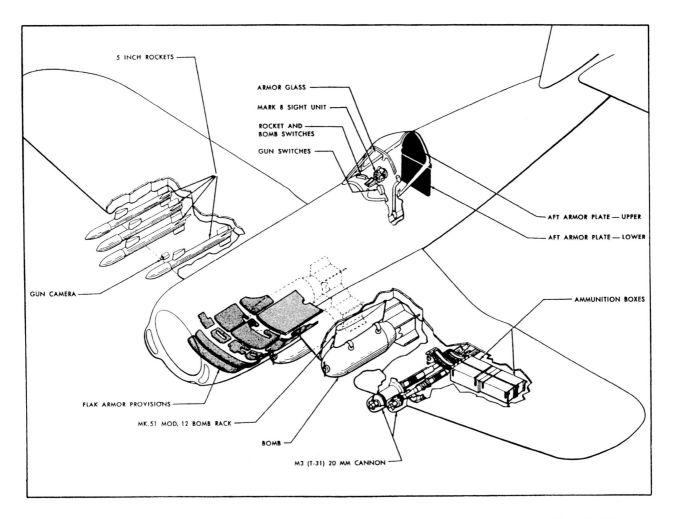

Although not as extensive as that installed in the AU-1 that followed, the F4U-5 had considerable flak armor protection beneath its engine compartment.

(U. S. Navy)

The F4U-5 was the first version of the Corsair to have metal skin on the outer wing panels where fabric had been used before.

(NMNA)

COCKPIT DETAILS

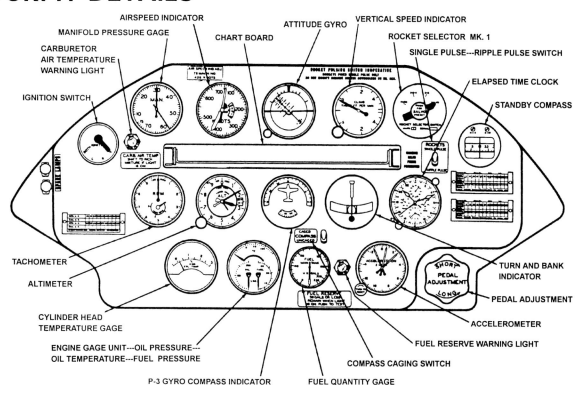

The main instrument panel in the F4U-5 was characterized by a slot for a chart board in its center. It did not have the lower panel that extended down between the rudder pedals as found on the F4U-4/-4B. (U. S. Navy)

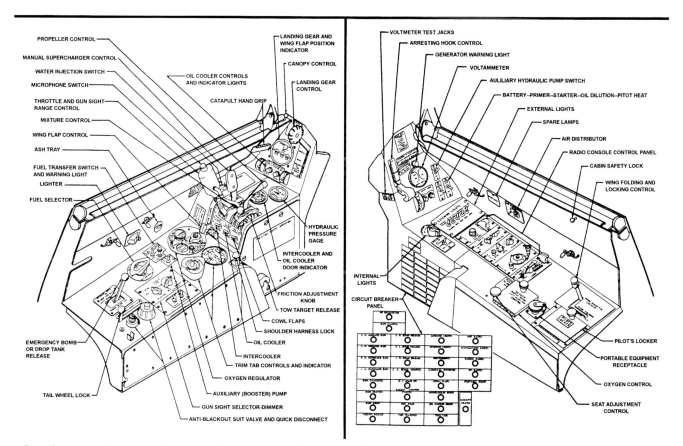

Details on the left console in an F4U-5 are identified in this drawing. The layout eliminated the conventional throttle quadrant, and the design was considerably different than that found in the F4U-4/-4B. (U. S. Navy)

The layout for the console on the right side of the cockpit was also very different than that used in the previous Corsair variant. However, many of the items located there remained the same. (U. S. Navy)

29

F4U-5P

Thirty F4U-5P photographic reconnaissance Corsairs were produced, and they carried the same armament as the standard F4U-5 day fighter. From this angle, the only way to determine that this was an F4U-5P was to notice the fairing on the vertical tail for the remote indicating compass transmitter. It is just visible immediately above the leading edge of the right wing. Extensions for the exhaust stubs were necessary to eliminate smudging on the oblique camera windows. **(NMNA)**

Thirty "dash 5" Corsairs were completed as F4U-5P photographic reconnaissance aircraft that could utilize the "K" series of cameras or the S-7S continuous strip camera. Unlike the F4U-4P, which had a camera window in

The fairing for the remote indicating compass transmitter is easier to see in this view. Also note that the F4U-5P had oblique camera windows on both sides of the fuselage instead of only the left as was the case on the F4U-4P. **(Vought)**

the bottom of the fuselage and on the left side, the F4U-5P had windows in the bottom and both sides of the fuselage. An easily recognizable identification feature of the F4U-5P was the fairing on the vertical tail that housed the remote indicating compass transmitter.

The vertical and oblique windows were covered by sliding doors which protected them from any leaking oil or hydraulic fluid when the cameras were not operating. Oil deflector rings were located on each of the doors. Exhaust stack extensions were also required to prevent the engine exhaust from distorting photographs taken through the oblique windows.

The "K" series of cameras could be rotated in flight to obtain photographs at ninety degrees through the vertical window in the bottom of the fuselage, or from three and fifteen degrees down from the horizontal through both oblique windows. Use of the S-7S camera required the installation of a scanner unit designed for that camera, a new door assembly in the lower fuselage at station 150, an amplifier unit under the turtledeck at station 223, and the installation of the S-7S camera remote control unit in the cockpit.

Although the F4U-5Ps had the same armament capability of the standard F4U-5 fighter, the mission requirements of these reconnaissance aircraft meant that they seldom, if ever, engaged in combat except for self-defense. Their job was to provide pre- or post-strike analysis of targets so that the fighters and bombers could do their jobs. F4U-5Ps did serve in Korea, but throughout most of the war, photo reconnaissance versions of the F9F Panther and F2H Banshee were also available. These jet aircraft, which could rely on their greater speed for increased protection, flew most Navy and Marine photo recon missions during the war.

COCKPIT DETAILS

The instrument panel in the F4U-5P was very similar to that in the standard F4U-5 day fighter. But some modification was necessary to add the intervalometer near the top and just inside the right eyebrow panel. Note that the F4U-5P retained the slot for the chart board at the center of the instrument panel. (Vought)

Except for a manual camera switch which was added just to the left of the throttle, the left console was identical to that in the F4U-5 day fighter. Note the heel rest on the rudder pedal that was designed to reduce pilot fatigue. The rest could be lowered to this position, or raised up out of the way as desired by the pilot. This feature was found in all "dash 5" Corsairs which had cockpits designed for pilot comfort and ease of operation. (Vought)

The console on the right side of the cockpit is shown here. The group of black knobs near the forward end of the flat part of the console is the camera control panel. The two small lights, right next to where the top of the console gets wider, are the camera interval warning and film feed indicator lights. About two inches aft of these lights are three switches. The one closest to the seat is the master camera switch, the middle one is the switch for the camera doors, and the outer one selects manual or automatic operation of the cameras. (Vought)

CAMERA INSTALLATION

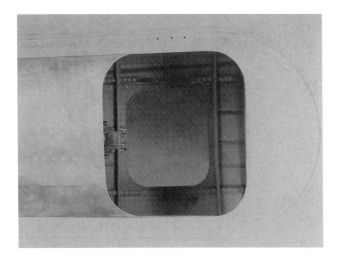

Although this factory photograph was taken before the aircraft was painted and is not of the highest quality, it shows the right side camera door cutout and the oil deflector ring. With no equipment installed in the camera bay, it is possible to look through it and out the camera window on the left side of the aircraft.   (Vought)

The right side camera door is shown here again in the open position from a slight angle. A K-17, 12-inch camera is installed in the vertical position.   (Vought)

Details of the K-17, 24-inch camera are shown here. The adapter for mounting it in the F4U-5P's camera bay is in place.   (Vought)

The shorter K-17, 12-inch camera looked like this with its adapter installed. The camera could be rotated in flight to allow it to take photographs through any of the three windows.   (Vought)

Coverage of the F4U-5 series of Corsairs continues on page 49.

COLOR GALLERY

F4U-4, USMC, China, 1945

This early F4U-4 had the curved windscreen and was flown by John H. Glenn, who later became a Mercury astronaut and U. S. Senator from Ohio. The national insignia used on Corsairs at the end of World War II still had the Insignia Blue surround on the overall Glossy Sea Blue paint scheme.

F4U-4, VF-783, USN

Typical of U. S. Navy markings used during the Korean War, this Corsair has the word NAVY painted on each side of the fuselage. A single-letter tail code was also common for most Navy aircraft. By this time, the red stripe had been added to the bars on each side of the national insignia, and the Insignia Blue surround had been deleted. This aircraft was assigned to the USS BON HOMME RICHARD, CV-31.

F4U-4, VMF-232, USMC

The U. S. Marine Corps lettered MARINE on the fuselage sides of most of its Corsairs and used two-letter tail codes. As with the Navy, aircraft numbers within the squadron were often painted on each side of the cowling, but at times, these numbers were located on the fuselage sides just forward of the national insignia.

F4U-4, MIAMI NAS, USNR

Beginning in the late 1940s, Corsairs assigned to the Navy Reserve usually had an orange band around the aft fuselage. The name of the Naval Air Station or Naval Reserve Air Station was often painted under the NAVY on the side of the fuselage.

F4U-5, VMF-212, USMC

F4U-5, BuNo, 122196, was flown by Major H. E. Smith of VMF-212 during 1952. The unit operated out of K-3 in Korea. MARINES was also lettered under the left wing, while the aircraft number and the tail code were usually on top of the right wing.

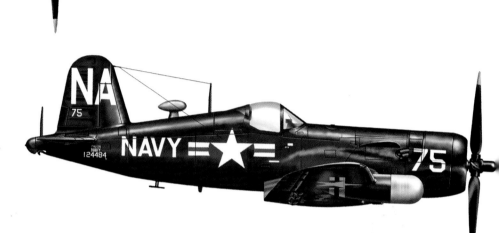

F4U-5N, VC-4, USN

This F4U-5N was assigned to VC-4 aboard the USS ANTIETAM, CV-36, in 1954. Navy composite squadrons, equipped with F4U-5Ns and the winterized -5NLs, used two-letter codes instead of the single-letter codes usually found on Navy aircraft during that time period.

F4U-5P, VMJ-1, USMC

Markings on Marine F4U-5P Corsairs were the same as those used on standard fighter versions. This F4U-5P was assigned to VMJ-1, and it saw service in Korea during February 1953.

AU-1, MCAS QUANTICO, USMC

A few Corsairs remained in service after the Navy and Marines began the change to the Light Gull Gray over white paint scheme. This AU-1 was assigned to Marine Corps Air Station, Quantico, Virginia, and it was one of the last Corsairs in operational service with the Marines. All lettering was flat black.

R-2800-32W ENGINE

The Pratt & Whitney R-2800-32W powerplant could be identified by its cylindrical crankcase with its numerous bolts. Note how far back the front row of cylinders is located inside the cowling.

This R-2800 is on display at the National Museum of Naval Aviation. Details of the cylindrical crankcase are easy to see, as are the two magnetos near the top of the crankcase. The top has been removed from one of the magnetos to reveal its interior.

A front view shows the correct colors for the crankcase, cylinders, pushrods, and wiring harness.

The display engine has been cut away on its right side to reveal interior details and the inner workings of the powerplant. Several cylinders have also been removed.

Pistons, pushrods, the crankcase, and other interior parts of the engine are visible through the cut away right side.

Details on the aft end of the R-2800-32W are shown in this photograph which was taken from behind and to the right of the powerplant.

F4U-4 COLORS

Above: An F4U-4 from VF-193 takes off from the USS PRINCETON, CV-37, in 1951. A 500-pound bomb can be seen on the left pylon under the center wing section, while smaller bombs are loaded on the wing pylons.
(Bennett via NMNA)

Left: This F4U-4 from VF-152 was also photographed aboard the USS PRINCETON, CV-37. Markings are typical for the Korean War period, and they include a single letter code on the vertical tail, the word NAVY in large white letters on each side of the fuselage with the squadron identification below it, the national insignia in four positions, and the aircraft number on each side of the cowling.
(Crohn via NMNA)

Below: Armed with rockets, bombs, and napalm, F4U-4s from VF-884 and VF-144 prepare to launch from the USS BOXER, CV-21, to strike communist targets on the Korean peninsular in 1951.
(NMNA)

Above: As their carrier turns into the wind, F4U-4s of VF-874 await the signal to launch for a mission in mid-1951. Note the pylons under the outer wing panels on the first aircraft, while the second Corsair in line has the zero-length rocket launchers. (NMNA)

Below: An F4U-4 from VF-63 folds its wings as it taxis forward after recovering aboard the USS PHILIPPINE SEA, CV-47. Standard markings on the top of the right wing included the aircraft's number and the single-letter tail code. (NMNA)

Above: The three photographs on this page all show Corsairs of VF-24 as that squadron operated aboard the USS PHILIPPINE SEA, CV-47, in 1951. Standard markings for Navy Corsairs during that time period are illustrated in these views. Here the pilot presses his head back against the headrest as the catapult officer gives the signal to launch. (Baker via NMNA)

Left: Another F4U-4 from VF-24 is brought up to the flight deck on the number two elevator with the pilot already in the cockpit. Note that the M code letter is repeated under the right wing. (Baker via NMNA)

Below: The aircraft number and code letter on top of the right wing are shown here. Also note that NAVY is painted under the left wing, and it is barely visible in this photograph. (Baker via NMNA)

Above: An F4U-4 from VMF-212 has been hooked up to the catapult aboard the USS BADOENG STRAIT, CVE-116, and is being checked over just prior to launch. Note how the hold-back cable is attached to the tail wheel assembly. F4U-4s were often fitted with one or two radio altimeter antennas under the aft fuselage.

(Haddock via NMNA)

Below: Further aft on the flight deck of the USS BADOENG STRAIT, more F4U-4s from VMF-212 prepare to launch. Most of the Corsairs are loaded with 5-inch rockets to attack targets in Korea. Note the mission markings painted on the right side of the forward fuselage on the aircraft which are spotted on the starboard side of the flight deck.

(Haddock via NMNA)

Above: With its wings extended, an F4U-4B from VMA-312 is chained to the flight deck aboard the USS BATAAN, CVL-29, while the light carrier makes a port call between assignments. (NMNA)

Left: Although elaborate nose art was relatively rare on Corsairs during the Korean War period, this F4U-4 from VMF-323 had a large rattlesnake painted on the cowling. The photograph was taken in June 1951 aboard the USS SICILY, CVE-118. (Yount via NMNA)

Below: In a setting typical of conditions during the warmer months in Korea, this F4U-4 from VMF-312 is loaded with 5-inch rockets and awaits its next mission against communist targets. (NMNA)

Above: An F4U-4P from HEDRON-2 makes a deck run to launch from the USS FRANKLIN D. ROOSEVELT, CVB-42. (NMNA)

Right: This F4U-4 was assigned to NAS Los Alamitos and has the typical orange fuselage band used on Naval Reserve aircraft. Note that the station name is also painted on the top of the right wing as well as the fuselage sides. (Melvin via NMNA)

Below: Honduras was one of several countries to operate Corsairs in the post-war years. National markings consisted of light blue and white stripes on the rudder and wing tips, but there was no other national insignia. Very similar rudder stripes were also used on Corsairs operated by El Salvador. (NMNA)

XF4U-4 COCKPIT DETAILS & COLORS

The layout of the instrument panel was conventional for U. S. Navy fighters designed during World War II.
(Webster)

The first XF4U-4 prototype, BuNo. 80759, is now on display at the New England Air Museum. The photographs on this page and the next illustrate the details in the cockpit of this Corsair. The unrestored paint provides an excellent reference for the colors used in the cockpits of F4U-4 Corsairs. This close-up provides a good look at the reflector gun sight. (Webster)

Unlike any previous Corsair variants, the XF4U-4, as well as the production F4U-4s and all subsequent versions, had a floor in the cockpit. The open area around the control column was usually covered with a canvas boot. The handle to the left is the hydraulic hand pump.
(Webster)

The XF4U-4 and production F4U-4s had a center panel between the rudder pedals. The two switches at the top were for charging the guns and were usually painted red. However, most of the red paint has worn off in this aircraft. Controls for the oil cooler and the vent for the cockpit cooling air were also on this panel. (Webster)

The XF4U-4 prototypes, as well as the production F4U-4s, were the first Corsairs to have a more conventional cockpit layout with full side consoles and a floor. Details of the left console are illustrated here. *(Webster)*

This close-up provides a detailed look at the throttle quadrant with its engine and propeller controls. The auxiliary panel just forward of the quadrant has controls for the landing gear and flaps as well as switches for the fuel pump. *(Webster)*

The seat used in the F4U-4 was quite different from ones used in earlier Corsairs. It had a bucket bottom, but the back was a separate piece of armor. *(Webster)*

Features on the right console are visible in this view. Circuit breakers were located on the side of the console. *(Webster)*

Above the seat back was another piece of armor with the head rest at the top. Full shoulder harnesses were once installed in the aircraft, but very little of them remains today. *(Webster)*

F4U-5 COLORS

Above: F4U-5s from VF-14 prepare for launch from the USS FRANKLIN D. ROOSEVELT, CVB-42, during the summer of 1953. By the time this photograph was taken, the wood planking, which originally covered the carrier's armored flight deck, had been removed. (NMNA)

Below: Harsh Korean winters often left aircraft on the flight decks of carriers covered with snow and ice. This F4U-5P was assigned to VC-61, and it shares the deck of the USS PHILIPPINE SEA, CV-47, with an F4U-5N and several Skyraiders. (Moffit via NMNA)

F4U-5N COLORS

Above: The most famous Corsair of the Korean War was this F4U-5N, BuNo. 124453, flown by Guy P. Bordelon, Jr. During the Korean War, Bordelon became the Navy's only ace, the only night fighter ace, and the only ace to fly a propeller-driven fighter. The white markings on the aircraft were covered over with a blue tint to reduced visibility at night. The aircraft was assigned to VC-3 which operated from the USS PRINCETON, CV-37. Modelers should note that there is no - between the VC and the 3 painted on the side of the fuselage below the NAVY. *(NMNA)*

Left: Standard markings for VC-3 aircraft are shown in this photograph that was taken aboard the USS VALLEY FORGE, CV-45, while the ship was in San Diego during November 1952. *(Shepard via NMNA)*

With his rudder kicked over to starboard to counter the torque of the engine, the pilot of an F4U-5N from VC-4 makes a deck run to take-off from the USS FRANKLIN D. ROOSEVELT, CVB-42. *(NMNA)*

VC-4's F4U-5Ns operated from the USS VALLEY FORGE, CV-45 during 1954. Three of the unit's night fighters are shown here being launched by catapult. *(Southerland via NMNA)*

F4U-5N DETAILS IN COLOR

F4U-5N, BuNo. 122189, was assigned to VMF(N)-513 and was painted in an overall flat black finish with red markings. With fire extinguisher in hand, a ground crewman watches the underside of the aircraft for fire as the pilot starts the engine for a mission from Kunson Air Base, Korea, in 1952. Today, the Marine Corps Museum at El Toro MCAS, California, has an F4U-5N that has been restored to represent this particular aircraft. The remaining photographs on this page and the next illustrate several of that aircraft's details. *(NMNA)*

A front view provides a good look at the Hamilton-Standard propeller, Pratt & Whitney R-2800-32W engine, and the cheek air scoops on the cowling. *(Jones)*

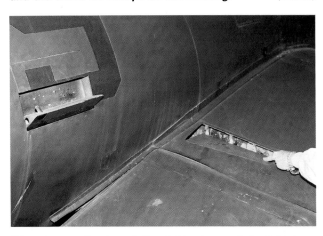

The step on the top of the right wing and the fold down step on the right side of the fuselage facilitated easy entry to the cockpit. *(Jones)*

Links and spent shells were ejected through slots under each wing. These are the slots under the left wing. The smaller slot for each cannon is for the links, while the larger slot is for the shells. *(Jones)*

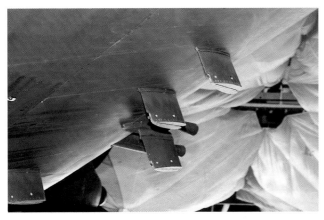

Stores carried under the outer wing panels were attached to stub pylons. Four pylons were mounted under each wing in a staggered arrangement, with one being located directly below the outboard cannon. These are the stub pylons under the right wing. Small bombs, up to the 250-pound size, and 5-inch rockets could be carried on these pylons. *(Jones)*

Two of the stub pylons under the left wing, including the one mounted directly beneath the outboard cannon, are shown here. The flash hiders on the cannon barrels were unique to the F4U-5N, and they were intended to prevent the pilot from being blinded by the flash of his cannons when they were fired at night. *(Jones)*

The APS-19A radar was housed in a fairing located on the leading edge of the right wing. *(Jones)*

Two radar altimeter antennas were located under the aft fuselage. This is a left side view of the aft antenna which was mounted just forward of the tail gear. A red beacon and a blade antenna can be seen just forward of the radio altimeter antenna. *(Jones)*

F4U-5Ns had a VHF antenna located on the tail cone just aft of the rudder. Another important feature in this photo is the trim tab on the elevator. The trim tab on all F4U-5 series Corsairs was completely different from the design used on all previous variants. A single tab was located on each elevator, and it was controlled by an actuator on the underside of the elevator. All previous Corsairs had a split tab arrangement with both a trim tab and a balance tab on each elevator. *(Jones)*

Details on the right side of the aft fuselage are visible here. Note the fold down step in the lower part of the 5. The door on this step could be folded closed when not in use. One of the antenna wires ran from the top of the vertical stabilizer to the top of the antenna mast, while the other entered the fuselage near the top of the national insignia. The tall tail gear is also visible in this photograph, although the tail gear doors have been removed from this aircraft. *(Jones)*

AU-1 COLORS

Above: This AU-1 was assigned to VMA-212. The arrow painted on each side of the fuselage was indicative of the squadron's nickname, "Lancers." On this particular aircraft, a replacement cowl flap has not been painted with a section of the arrow. The photograph was taken in Japan during 1952. (Jay via NMNA)

Left: A few Navy and Marine AU-1s remained in service after the change to the Light Gull Gray over white paint scheme had begun. Also see the side profile of a Marine AU-1 in this paint scheme on page 34. (Starinchank via NMNA)

Below: Typical of Navy Reserve Corsairs, this AU-1 from NAS Akron has the orange band around its fuselage. It was photographed at Knoxville, Tennessee, in September 1956. (NMNA)

F4U-5N & F4U-5NL

With a considerable amount of yellow paint on its undersides, this F4U-5N was used as a test aircraft. It is missing the flash hiders on the cannon barrels and the stub pylons under the wings. (U. S. Navy via Jones)

The majority of "dash 5" Corsairs were completed as night fighters, with a total of 315 being produced. This

Most Corsairs in the "dash 5" series were completed as F4U-5N or F4U-5NL night fighters. They were characterized by the radome on the leading edge of the right wing. Also note the flash hiders on the cannons. (NMNA)

compares to only 223 F4U-5 day fighters and 30 F4U-5P photographic reconnaissance aircraft. The night fighters were divided into two sub-variants including 214 F4U-5Ns and 101 F4U-5NLs. The F4U-5NL differed from the F4U-5N only in that it had special winterization equipment that permitted it to operate effectively in extremely cold climatic conditions like those in Korea. This winterization equipment included a windscreen deicer and deicing boots on the leading edges of the wings and tail surfaces.

The night fighter equipment found on both the F4U-5N and F4U-5NL included an AN/APS-19 or -19A radar set mounted in a large fairing on the leading edge of the right wing, a P-1 auto pilot, AN/ARC-28 communications (VHF) equipment, and AN/APX-2 IFF equipment. The night fighters also had an AN/APN-1 radio altimeter, a windshield degreaser, and a Mk 20 gun sight. To help protect the pilot's vision at night, T-20 flash hiders were added to the muzzles of the cannon barrels, flame hiders were mounted above the upper exhaust on each side of the fuselage, and exhaust collector flame dampeners were added to the ends of the exhaust stubs. The throttle ranging grip, found in the standard F4U-5, was replaced with a conventional throttle grip and microphone switch in the night fighters. The scope for the radar was mounted in the center of the main instrument panel.

For night fighter gunnery training, a special light, mounted on the leading edge of the right wing next to the gun camera, was used with trihedral prism retro-reflectors. One of these was mounted on top of each wing near the trailing edge of the tip, and one was located on

49

The flat black deicing boots on the leading edge of the wings indicate that this is a winterized F4U-5NL. Although not clearly visible in the photograph, deicing boots were also on the leading edge of the vertical and horizontal stabilizers. This aircraft is from VC-4, and the pilot's name stencilled on the side of the fuselage reads, ENS. CAWLEY. *Details on the flight deck indicate that this is one of the three MIDWAY class carriers.*

(U. S. Navy via Jones)

F4U-5 and -5NL night fighters flew most of their missions in Korea attacking targets on the ground. Here, an F4U-5N of VMF(N)-513's Flying Nightmares is refueled between missions. *(NMNA)*

each side of the tail cone. During training exercises at night, the pilot would press his gun trigger, and instead of the cannons firing, the light would shine a beam at the target. If the pilot's "shooting" was on target, the light would reflect from all of the trihedral prisms. If the pilot was off target, the light would not reflect from all of the prisms. The gun camera would record the results of the mock attack.

The most famous Corsair pilot of the Korean War was Guy Bordelon who became the Navy's only ace of that conflict. His five aerial victories were scored in an F4U-5N while he was assigned to VC-3. Bordelon was also the only night fighter ace and the only ace to fly a propeller-driven aircraft during that conflict.

While the F4U-5N and -5NL Corsairs did fly missions in their intended night fighter role, they also flew hundreds of ground attack sorties against communist targets. Their external armament capabilities were the same as the standard F4U-5, so they were equally as effective in that role as well.

By the time the Korean War was over, the days of the propeller-driven night fighters were all but over. Navy and Marine F4U-5Ns and -5NLs were replaced by the jet powered F3D Skyknights, but a few were sold to Honduras and Argentina. By the end of the decade, almost all fighters were radar equipped, allowing them to operate in all weather conditions and as effectively at night as during the day. As a result, the distinction between day fighter and night fighter gradually disappeared.

COCKPIT DETAILS

The main difference between the instrument panel in the night fighters and the standard F4U-5 day fighters was the radar scope located at the center of the panel just below the gun sight. *(Vought)*

The photographs on this page were taken in BuNo. 124724, which was the last F4U-5N/-5NL that was built. The addition of the radar scope caused the chart board to be eliminated from the instrument panel. *(Vought)*

Above: The side consoles were almost the same as in the F4U-5 day fighter. This close-up of the forward end of the left console shows the engine controls and the landing gear lever to good effect. Most noteworthy is the extended throttle handle. *(Vought)*

Center right: The right console was covered with switches, most of them being related to electrical equipment including the radios. Circuit breakers remained on the side of the console forward of the seat. *(Vought)*

Right: Radio gear and other electrical equipment was housed in the fuselage immediately aft of the cockpit. *(Vought)*

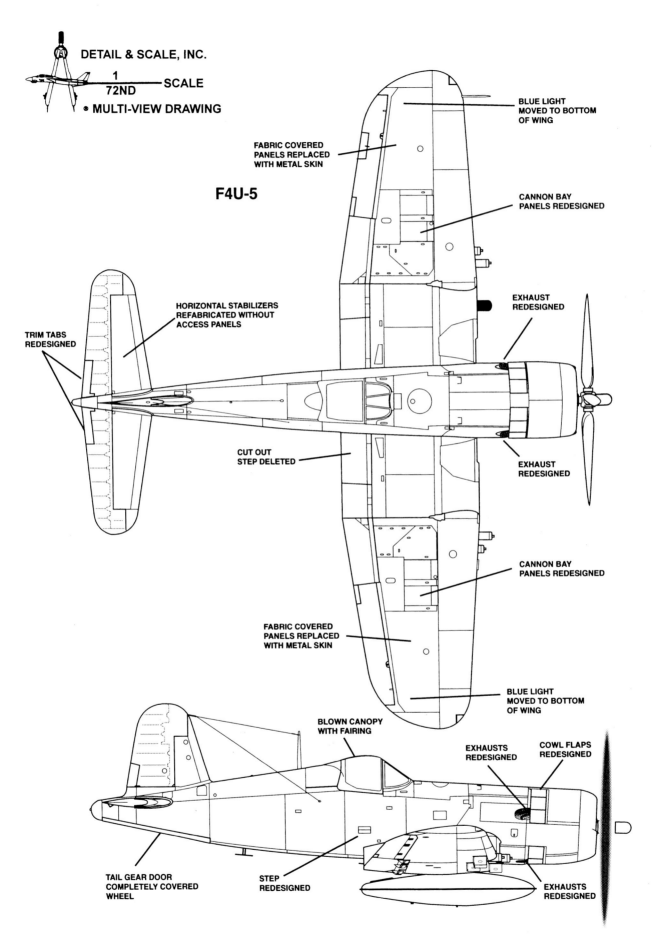

DETAIL & SCALE, INC.

$\frac{1}{72ND}$ SCALE

• MULTI-VIEW DRAWING

F4U-5

FABRIC COVERED
PANELS REPLACED
WITH METAL SKIN

BLUE LIGHT
MOVED TO BOTTOM
OF WING

CANNON BAY
PANELS REDESIGNED

HORIZONTAL STABILIZERS
REFABRICATED WITHOUT
ACCESS PANELS

EXHAUST
REDESIGNED

TRIM TABS
REDESIGNED

CUT OUT
STEP DELETED

EXHAUST
REDESIGNED

CANNON BAY
PANELS REDESIGNED

FABRIC COVERED
PANELS REPLACED
WITH METAL SKIN

BLUE LIGHT
MOVED TO BOTTOM
OF WING

BLOWN CANOPY
WITH FAIRING

EXHAUSTS
REDESIGNED

COWL FLAPS
REDESIGNED

TAIL GEAR DOOR
COMPLETELY COVERED
WHEEL

STEP
REDESIGNED

EXHAUSTS
REDESIGNED

DETAIL & SCALE COPYRIGHT © DRAWINGS BY LLOYD S. JONES

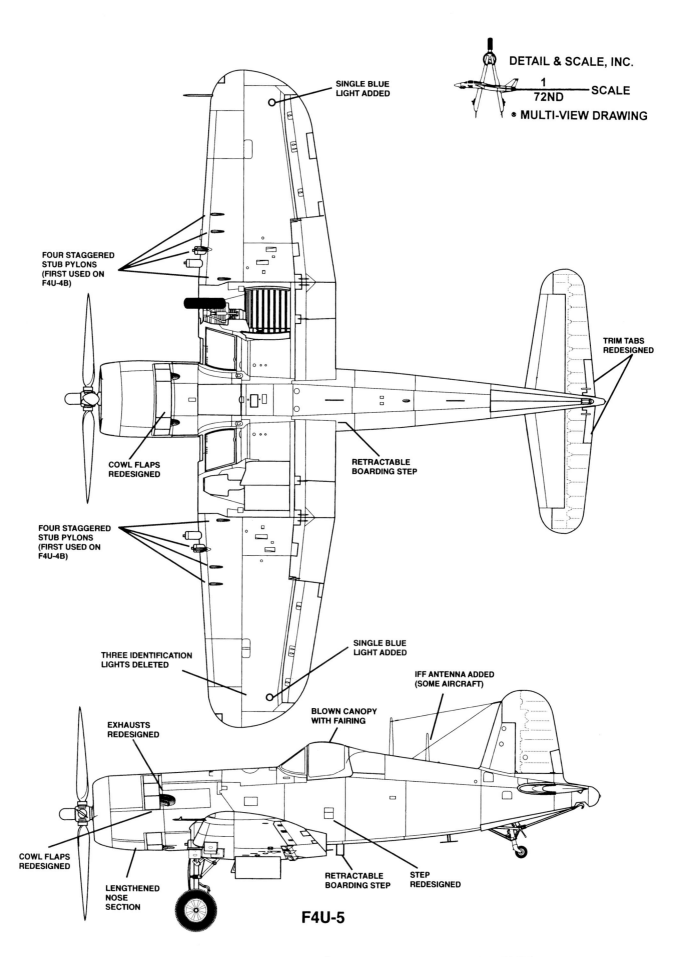

SINGLE BLUE LIGHT ADDED

DETAIL & SCALE, INC.
1
72ND
SCALE
® MULTI-VIEW DRAWING

FOUR STAGGERED STUB PYLONS (FIRST USED ON F4U-4B)

TRIM TABS REDESIGNED

COWL FLAPS REDESIGNED

RETRACTABLE BOARDING STEP

FOUR STAGGERED STUB PYLONS (FIRST USED ON F4U-4B)

THREE IDENTIFICATION LIGHTS DELETED

SINGLE BLUE LIGHT ADDED

IFF ANTENNA ADDED (SOME AIRCRAFT)

EXHAUSTS REDESIGNED

BLOWN CANOPY WITH FAIRING

COWL FLAPS REDESIGNED

LENGTHENED NOSE SECTION

RETRACTABLE BOARDING STEP

STEP REDESIGNED

F4U-5

DETAIL & SCALE COPYRIGHT © DRAWINGS BY LLOYD S. JONES

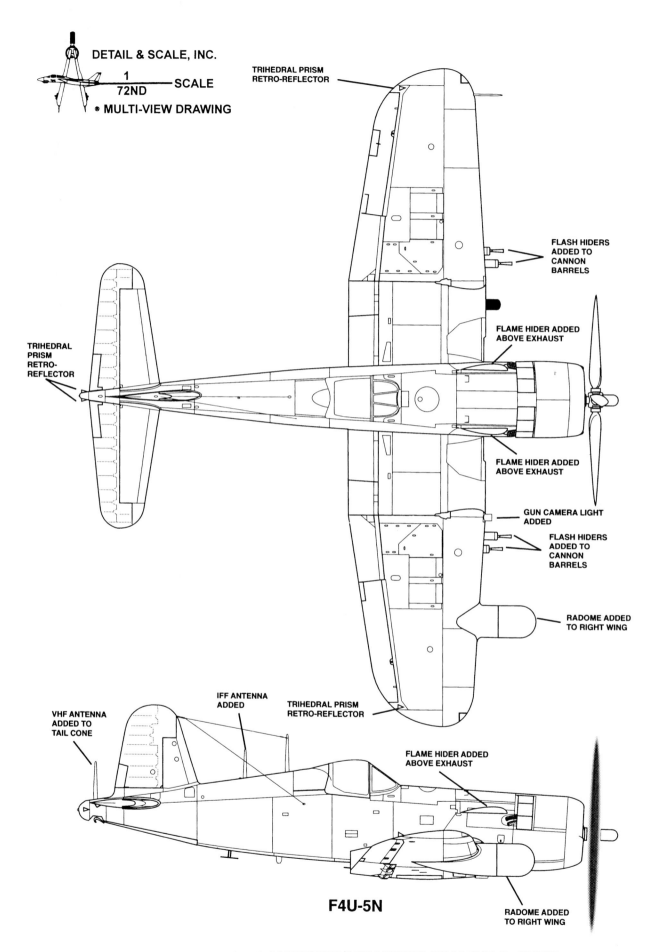

DETAIL & SCALE, INC.

1
72ND ── SCALE

® MULTI-VIEW DRAWING

TRIHEDRAL PRISM
RETRO-REFLECTOR

FLASH HIDERS
ADDED TO
CANNON
BARRELS

FLAME HIDER ADDED
ABOVE EXHAUST

TRIHEDRAL
PRISM
RETRO-
REFLECTOR

FLAME HIDER ADDED
ABOVE EXHAUST

GUN CAMERA LIGHT
ADDED

FLASH HIDERS
ADDED TO
CANNON
BARRELS

RADOME ADDED
TO RIGHT WING

VHF ANTENNA
ADDED TO
TAIL CONE

IFF ANTENNA
ADDED

TRIHEDRAL PRISM
RETRO-REFLECTOR

FLAME HIDER ADDED
ABOVE EXHAUST

F4U-5N

RADOME ADDED
TO RIGHT WING

DETAIL & SCALE COPYRIGHT © DRAWINGS BY LLOYD S. JONES

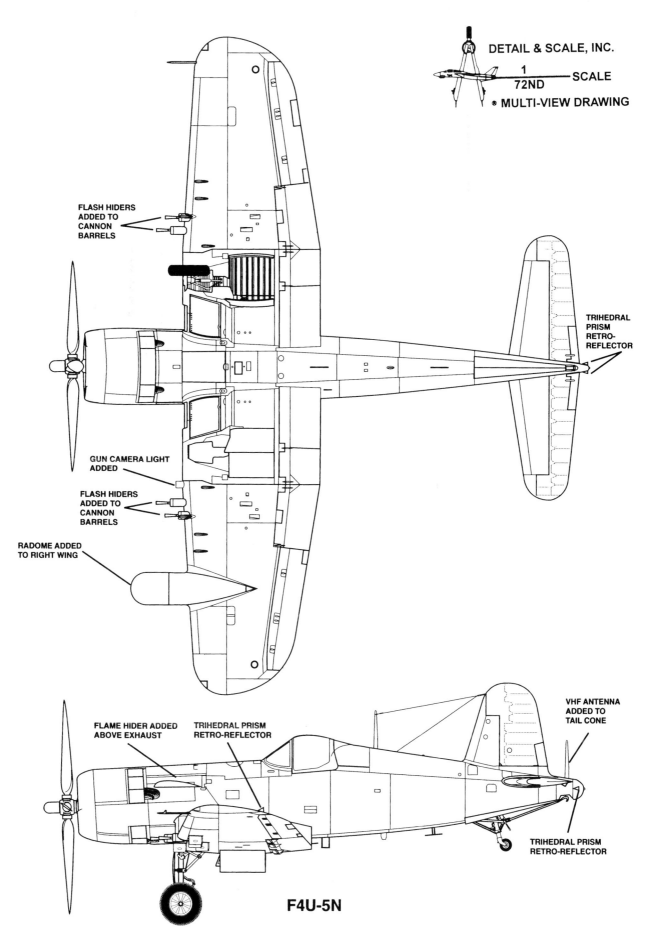

FLASH HIDERS
ADDED TO
CANNON
BARRELS

TRIHEDRAL
PRISM
RETRO-
REFLECTOR

GUN CAMERA LIGHT
ADDED

FLASH HIDERS
ADDED TO
CANNON
BARRELS

RADOME ADDED
TO RIGHT WING

FLAME HIDER ADDED
ABOVE EXHAUST

TRIHEDRAL PRISM
RETRO-REFLECTOR

VHF ANTENNA
ADDED TO
TAIL CONE

TRIHEDRAL PRISM
RETRO-REFLECTOR

F4U-5N

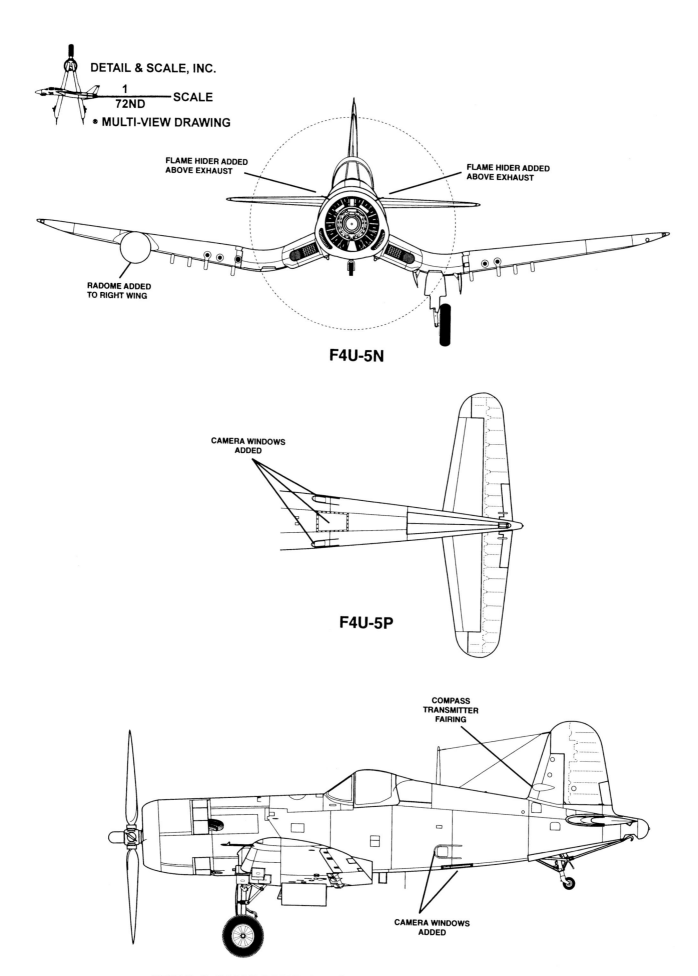

DETAIL & SCALE, INC.

$\dfrac{1}{72ND}$ SCALE

• MULTI-VIEW DRAWING

FLAME HIDER ADDED
ABOVE EXHAUST

FLAME HIDER ADDED
ABOVE EXHAUST

RADOME ADDED
TO RIGHT WING

F4U-5N

CAMERA WINDOWS
ADDED

F4U-5P

COMPASS
TRANSMITTER
FAIRING

CAMERA WINDOWS
ADDED

DETAIL & SCALE COPYRIGHT © DRAWINGS BY LLOYD S. JONES

F4U-5 DETAILS
WINDSCREEN, CANOPY, & COCKPIT ENTRY

NOTE: On this and the next eight pages are photographs of details common to the F4U-5 series of Corsairs. Unless otherwise indicated, these details apply to all sub-variants in the "dash 5" series including the F4U-5, F4U-5N, F4U-5NL, and F4U-5P.

The windscreen on the F4U-5 series was the flat design used on most F4U-4s. Notice how close the two forward frames are at the top. Modelers should note that most Corsair kits have these frames too far apart.

All "dash 5" Corsairs had a blown canopy that afforded better visibility to the rear. The amount the canopy was bulged is quite noticeable from behind.

Above: The canopy was also higher, and this necessitated the addition of a fairing on the spine of the fuselage. When closed, the top of the canopy's aft framework sealed against this fairing.

Right: The cut out step in the inner right flap, which had been standard on late F4U-1Ds and all F4U-4/-4Bs, was eliminated on the F4U-5. Instead, a retractable boarding step was installed just aft of the trailing edge of the right wing. A fold down step was located higher on the side of the fuselage.

LANDING GEAR DETAILS

A factory photograph shows the left main gear on an F4U-5. The wheel is the spoked design used on Corsairs and Hellcats throughout most of their operational life, and the tire has the diamond tread pattern. (Vought)

This solid wheel was used on Corsairs and Hellcats late in their operational service, but it appears to have been used on more Hellcats than Corsairs.

Details on the inside of the left main gear are visible in this photograph. Note the tie-down ring on the front of the strut.

A rear view of the left landing gear provides an excellent look at the main strut. Note the brake line running down the strut to the inside of the wheel. (Jones)

TAIL LANDING GEAR

The F4U-5 was the first Corsair to have tail landing gear doors that completely covered the retracted wheel. A small bulge was near the center of the doors to permit them to be closed over the tire.

When open, the tail gear doors were almost parallel to the ground rather than hanging down from the fuselage. The tire in this photograph, and the one to the left, is the pneumatic tire usually used for land-based operations.

With the tail of the aircraft up on jacks, the tail gear assembly is completely visible. As with the case on other Corsair variants, the arresting hook was part of this assembly. This gear has the hard rubber tire usually used for carrier operations. (Vought)

Details on the insides of the tail gear doors can be seen here. This photograph was taken just to the right of the tail gear, and it looks aft at the open doors.

COWLING & EXHAUST DETAILS

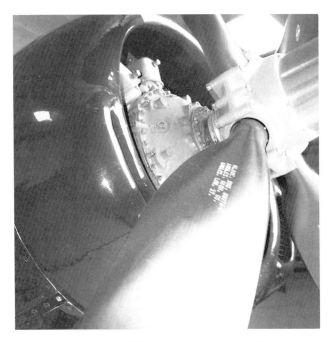

Above left and right: The two cheek-mounted scoops on the lip of the cowling are shown in these two views. Details on the engine crankcase are also visible.

The two upper exhausts were located higher on each side of the fuselage than they had been on the F4U-4. This photograph was taken on an F4U-5N, and the flash hider, found only on the night fighters, can be seen just above the exhausts. Also note the area on the side of the fuselage where there were no cowl flaps. This was a completely different design than found on any previous Corsair variants.

Like the F4U-4, the F4U-5 had a single exhaust stub on each side of the lower cowling. This is the lower stub on the right side.

The lower left exhaust stub can be seen in this view that looks into the open cooling flaps. Note how the cooling flaps go all the way around the bottom of the cowling.

FUSELAGE & PYLON DETAILS

Although the cooling flaps on the F4U-5 were redesigned, they did not go all the way across the top of the fuselage. This was to prevent engine oil from seeping out at the top and blowing back onto the windscreen. The filler for the internal fuel tank is also visible in this photograph.

This interesting shot looks into the forward fuselage section prior to it being joined to the aft section. Note how the interior of the fuselage was painted flat black and Chromate Green. (Vought)

Access to the radio compartment was gained through a door on the right side of the fuselage. It was located just aft of the retractable boarding step. (Vought)

An unusual centerline pylon was added to the F4U-5, and it was also used on the AU-1 and F4U-7 that followed. In this view, an 11.75-inch rocket is attached to the pylon. Note how the pylon had a cut out area that permitted the operation of the vent door for the intercooler and engine accessory compartment. (Vought)

This close-up shows how a bomb would be attached to the centerline pylon. Bombs up to the 2,000-pound size could be carried on this station. (Vought)

WING DETAILS

As with all Corsairs, the F4U-5 series had both a balance tab and a trim tab on the left aileron. The balance tab is the one at the inboard end of the aileron, while the trim tab is located further out on the aileron.

The right aileron had the balance tab at its inboard end, but it did not have a trim tab.

The three flap sections on each wing were the same as they had been on all previous Corsairs. These are the flaps on the left wing.

The flaps on the right wing are illustrated here. No Corsairs from the F4U-5 on had the cut out step in the inner right flap.

The wing fold area was cluttered with the main hinge, flap actuators, hydraulic lines, control lines, and electrical wires. (Vought)

The oil cooler and intercooler inlets in the wing roots remained the same as they had been on previous Corsairs.

The panels that covered the 20-mm cannons and their ammunition boxes were a different design than that used on Corsairs that were armed with six .50-caliber machine guns. Also note that the entire wing surface was covered with a metal skin. All previous Corsair variants had fabric covering over much of the outer wing panels.

The gun camera window was located on the leading edge of the right wing just inboard of the cannons.

The vent door for the right oil cooler and intercooler intake is shown here in the lowered position. Note the small cutout on the trailing edge of the vent door to allow it to clear the pylon. The right catapult bridle hook is also visible.

Details of the left pylon under the center wing section are shown here from below and slightly in front. Also note the catapult bridle hook just inboard of the pylon at its leading edge.

The three identification lights, which had been standard on all previous versions of the Corsair, were eliminated on the F4U-5. Instead, the single blue light, that had previously been on top of each wing, was moved to the underside as shown here.

TAIL DETAILS

Earlier Corsairs had trim tabs on their rudders that were controlled by an actuator on the left side. *The actuator on the rudder of the F4U-5 was located at the bottom of the trim tab. Note the counterbalance on the arm of the actuator.*

As on the F4U-4, antenna wires on the F4U-5 were attached to the point at the top of the vertical stabilizer rather than to a stub mast on the rudder.

A clear light was located on the aft end of the tail cone.

Each elevator had a single trim tab that was electrically controlled. The actuator for each tab was on the lower surface of the elevator. This was a completely different arrangement than used on any previous Corsair variant.

AU-1

Although it had originally been called the XF4U-6, the designation for the prototype for the final U. S. version of the Corsair was changed to XAU-1 before it was delivered. This prototype was converted from F4U-5N, BuNo. 124665, and it made its initial flight on January 31, 1952. It is shown here shortly after the conversion was completed, and its ten outer wing pylons were loaded with bombs.   *(U. S. Navy via Jones)*

Originally designated the XF4U-6, the AU-1 was a dedicated ground attack variant developed from the F4U-

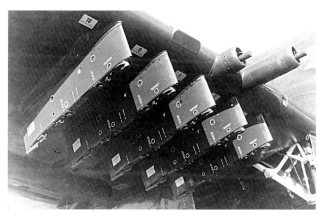

This close-up provides a good look at the five pylons under the right wing. Note that the pylons are numbered from one to ten from left to right. These pylons could be loaded with bombs up to the 500-pound size, but if 500-pound bombs were used, their diameter meant that only the inboard, center, and outboard pylons under each wing could be used. Smaller bombs of the 250-pound class could be loaded on all five pylons as seen in the photograph at the top of this page. A five-inch rocket could also be carried on each pylon. The ordnance carrying capability of the two pylons under the center wing section and that of the centerline station remained the same as it had been on the F4U-5.   *(Vought)*

5. It retained the metal skinned outer wing panels of the "dash 5" series, and it had the blown canopy with the fairing directly behind it. Contrary to information published elsewhere, its service was not limited to the U. S. Marine Corps, although most were assigned to the Marines. Twenty-five Marine AU-1s were turned over to the French for use in Indochina, while others did serve with the U. S. Navy as well.

F4U-5N, BuNo. 124665, was converted to the sole XF4U-6 prototype, and it first flew on January 31, 1952, after having been redesignated the XAU-1. Deliveries of the 111 production AU-1s were made between February 7 and October 10, 1952. BuNos. were 129318 through 129417, and 133833 through 133843.

Because a ground attack aircraft is not expected to fly at high altitudes, the two-stage, variable-speed supercharger used on the F4U-5 was not needed. Instead, the AU-1 was fitted with an R-2800-83W which had a single-stage, manually controlled supercharger instead. But the longer fuselage of the F4U-5 was retained, and even the bulges on the sides of the forward fuselage remained where they had been on the F4U-5. The R-2800-83W (also designated the R-2800-83WA), with its single-stage supercharger, did not require the two cheek scoops, so these were deleted. However, when viewed from the front, the cowl ring of the AU-1 still had the bulges where the scoops had been on the F4U-5.

Five pylons were installed under each outer wing panel, and 5-inch rockets, 100-pound bombs, or 250-pound bombs could be carried on each. If only the inner, middle, and outer pylon on each wing was used, 500-pound bombs could be loaded. The AU-1 also retained the two pylons under the center wing section as well as the centerline station as found on the F4U-5. The gun armament remained the four 20-mm cannon used in all Corsairs from the F4U-4B on, although they received some modification for use in the AU-1. This allowed them to all be fired together or in pairs. By using only one cannon in each wing at a time, firepower was cut in half, but firing time was doubled. The longer firing time often

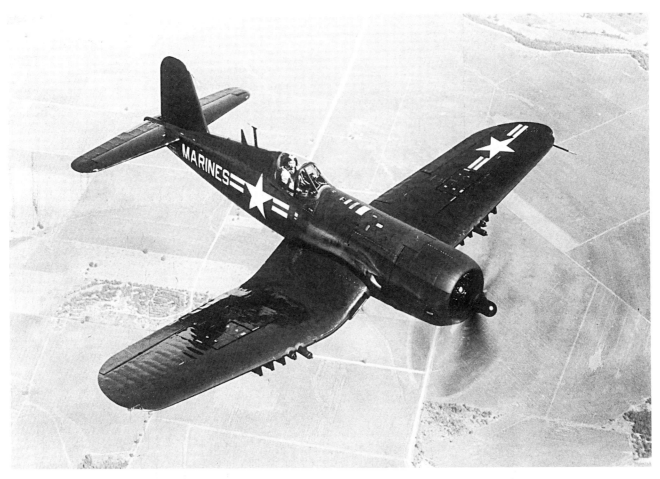

This flying shot of an early AU-1 provides a good look at the aircraft's features. It should be noted that, although the AU-1 had the longer fuselage of the F4U-5, the upper exhausts on each side were in the lower position as found on the F4U-4. (NMNA)

proved much more valuable in ground support or RESCAP operations.

To make the aircraft more survivable in the hostile environment of anti-aircraft fire encountered when operating at low altitudes, twenty-five pieces of armor were added to protect the engine, fuel tanks, and cockpit. The oil coolers were repositioned so that they no longer faced forward. Instead, they were mounted in the wing roots facing inboard. The air entered the wing scoops as before, but ducting routed it to the oil coolers. This design change protected the oil coolers from ground fire coming from the front of the aircraft and also increased protection from fire coming from below.

AU-1s were used by several Marine squadrons in Korea during the second half of the war. They remained in Marine service until 1957, a year after they had been retired by the Navy Reserves. A few continued to serve with the French Navy until 1964.

Covered with snow, an AU-1 assigned to NAS Minneapolis, Minnesota, displays the orange fuselage band common on U. S. Naval Reserve aircraft in the 1950s. (NMNA)

Among the last Corsairs in U. S. service were those at MCAS Quantico, Virginia. They were painted in the Light Gull Gray over white paint scheme that replaced the overall Gloss Sea Blue scheme which had been applied to Corsairs since early 1945. (NMNA)

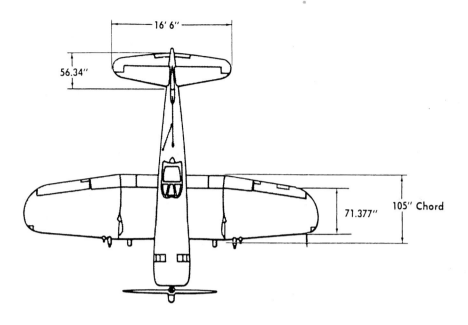

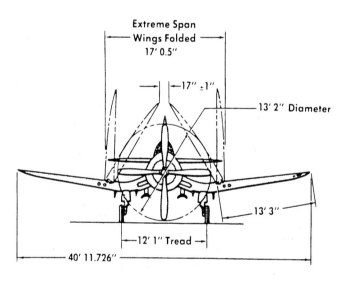

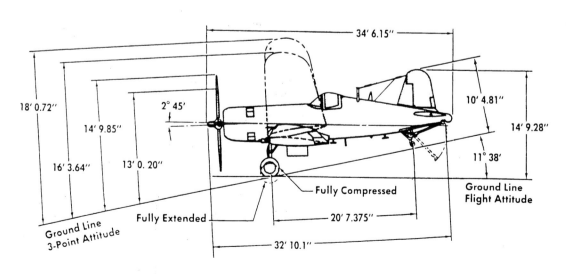

This drawing was taken from the official Navy maintenance manual for the AU-1. It clearly shows that the AU-1 had the longer fuselage length of 33' 6.15" like the F4U-5 series of Corsairs.

(U. S. Navy)

COCKPIT DETAILS

The instrument panel in the AU-1 was different from that in the previous F4U-5, and it did not have the slot for the chart board. This is the panel in the first production AU-1 to come off the assembly line. (Vought)

Details on the left side of the cockpit are shown in this photograph that was taken while the aircraft was still under construction. (Vought)

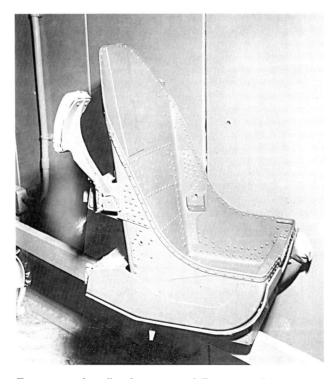

To protect the pilot from ground fire, a special armored seat was installed in the AU-1. (Vought)

Here is a look at the right side of the cockpit in an AU-1. As with other late Corsair variants, the cockpit was painted flat black except for the floor, control column, and seat, which were Chromate Green. (Vought)

ENGINE DETAILS

This view looks over the top of the R-2800-83W powerplant used in the AU-1. *(Vought)*

Details on the right side of the engine assembly are shown here. *(Vought)*

The upper exhausts on the left side are visible in this photograph which was taken after the engine assembly had been joined with the fuselage. *(Vought)*

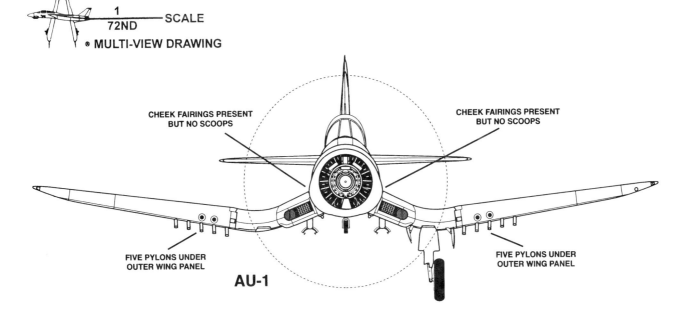

DETAIL & SCALE, INC.

1
——— SCALE
72ND

® MULTI-VIEW DRAWING

CHEEK FAIRINGS PRESENT BUT NO SCOOPS

CHEEK FAIRINGS PRESENT BUT NO SCOOPS

FIVE PYLONS UNDER OUTER WING PANEL

FIVE PYLONS UNDER OUTER WING PANEL

AU-1

DETAIL & SCALE COPYRIGHT © DRAWING BY LLOYD S. JONES

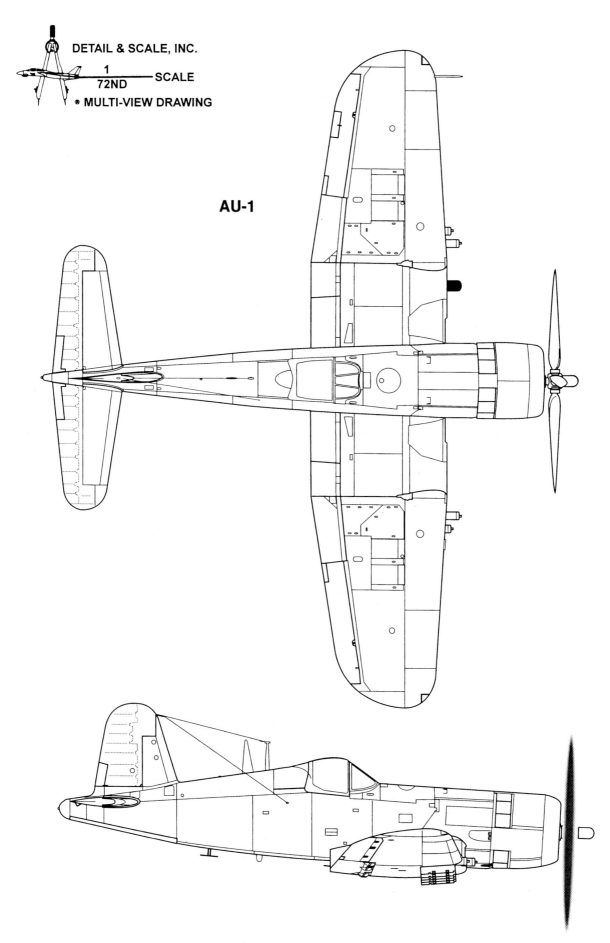

AU-1

DETAIL & SCALE, INC.

$\frac{1}{72ND}$ SCALE

● MULTI-VIEW DRAWING

DETAIL & SCALE COPYRIGHT © DRAWINGS BY LLOYD S. JONES

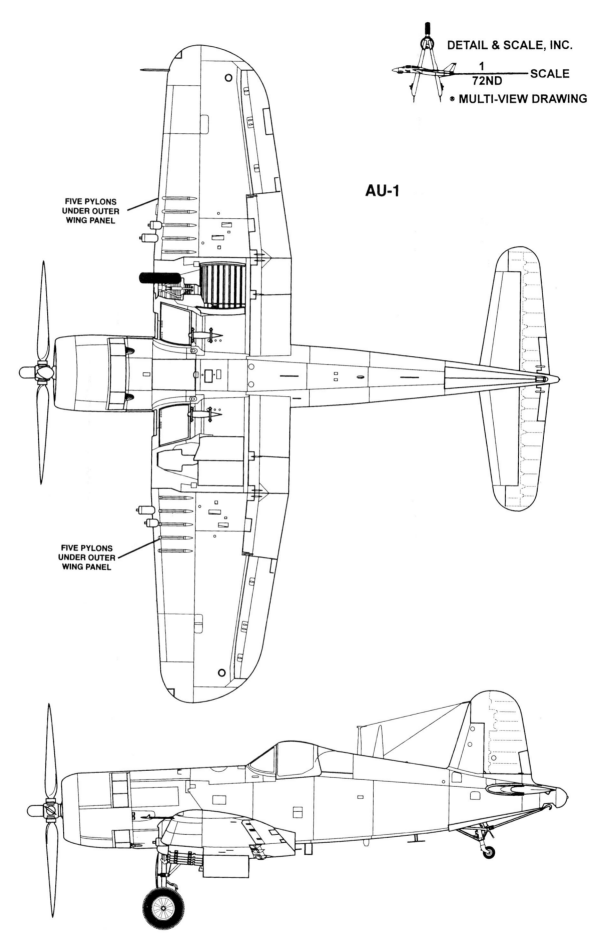

DETAIL & SCALE, INC.

$\dfrac{1}{72ND}$ —— SCALE

® MULTI-VIEW DRAWING

AU-1

FIVE PYLONS
UNDER OUTER
WING PANEL

FIVE PYLONS
UNDER OUTER
WING PANEL

DETAIL & SCALE COPYRIGHT © DRAWINGS BY LLOYD S. JONES

F4U-7

The F4U-7 was the last Corsair variant to be produced, and ninety-four were delivered to the French Navy in 1952 and early 1953. The F4U-7 was powered by The R-2800-43W engine used in later F4U-4s and F4U-4Bs, and it had physical features in common with the F4U-4B, F4U-5, and the AU-1. *(Vought via Jones)*

Like the AU-1, the F4U-7 had ten pylons under the outer wing panels. Some of these French Corsairs were modified so that SS-11 air-to-surface missiles could be launched from these pylons. *(NMNA)*

The French F4U-7 became the last Corsair variant to be produced. The first of these made its initial flight on July 2, 1952, and deliveries of the ninety-four aircraft were concluded by the end of January the following year. These aircraft carried U. S. Navy Bureau numbers 133652 through 133731, and 133819 through 133832. F4U-7s remained in service with the French Navy for eleven years until 1964. During that time they were assigned to the 12th, 14th, 15th, and 17th Flotilles.

Much misinformation has been published about the features of the F4U-7. It was a cross between the F4U-4B and the AU-1, but it did not have the longer fuselage of the AU-1 as recently reported in another publication. Instead, the F4U-7 had the same 33' 8.25" fuselage length of the F4U-4 and F4U-4B. The F4U-7 had the higher blown canopy, and its related fairing on the spine of the fuselage as found on the F4U-5 and AU-1. There has also been some conflicting reports as to what engine was used in the French Corsairs. The powerplant used in this variant was the R-2800-43W, first installed in later F4U-4s and F4U-4Bs. As a result, the F4U-7 also had the chin scoop at the bottom of the cowl ring.

To carry external stores, the F4U-7 had the AU-1's five pylons under each outer wing section to carry rockets and small bombs. Some F4U-7s were also equipped to

launch SS-11 air-to-surface missiles. They retained the two pylons under the center wing section, and there was also a centerline station as well. Standard internal armament was four 20-mm cannon mounted in the wings as found on the F4U-4B and all subsequent U. S. versions.

During their operational service, the French F4U-7s flew from land bases and the aircraft carriers LAFAYETTE, ARROMANCHES, and BOIS BELLEAU. They participated in combat in Algeria and the Suez Canal area. French Corsairs also took part in the fighting in Indochina, but they were the twenty-five AU-1s provided to the French in April 1954, rather than the F4U-7s.

F4U-7s were assigned to Flotilles 12, 14, 15, and 17 in the Aeronavale. This Corsair was assigned to 12 Flotille as indicated by the 12F painted on its fuselage. (NMNA)

One of the few surviving F4U-7s is now on display at Battleship Park in Mobile, Alabama. However, it is erroneously painted as an AU-1 from VMA-212. This photograph shows the centerline pylon and the two pylons under the center wing section loaded with bombs. Note how the vent door for the intercooler and engine accessory compartment lowered into the cut out area of the centerline pylon.

An F4U-7 from 14 Flotille takes off from the French aircraft carrier BOIS BELLEAU. This ship was the former U. S. light carrier, USS BELLEAU WOOD, CVL-24. (NMNA)

MODELERS SECTION

Note: The kit reviews included in this Modelers Section are for injection molded plastic kits of the Corsair variants covered in this book. These include the F4U-4 through the F4U-7. For reviews of the earlier Corsair versions, see The F4U Corsair in Detail & Scale, Part 1, Detail & Scale, Volume 55. It should also be noted that no kits have been produced in 1/144th scale or 1/32nd scale for the F4U-4 through the F4U-7 versions.

1/72nd SCALE KITS

Fujimi F4U-4/-4B

Only two 1/72nd scale kits of the F4U-4/-4B have been issued, and this one is no longer available. It was very poor, detailing was lacking throughout, and much of what was provided was incorrect.

Simply stated, this is a very inaccurate kit that cannot be used to build an authentic model of the F4U-4. Therefore, modelers wanting to build a 1/72nd scale F4U-4 or F4U-4B would be better off using the Matchbox kit.

Fujimi F4U-5N

This is essentially the same kit as the F4U-4B issue covered above. The only changes made to the plastic were the addition of the radome for the right wing and a different cowl ring with the two cheek scoops. These are by no means all of the changes required to make any "dash 5" series Corsair. As a result, the cowl flaps are wrong, because the ones on the real F4U-5 were quite different from the ones on the F4U-4. The lengthened nose section is also not represented, and the fairings on the sides for the cheek scoops are also missing. The exhausts are incorrect for an F4U-5, and the F4U-5N's exhaust glare shields are not provided.

All of the other problems found in the F4U-4B issue covered above are present in this kit as well. Therefore, we cannot recommend this kit, and we suggest using the much better Italeri 1/72nd scale F4U-5N instead.

Hawk AU-1

Although the box art claims that this model is an AU-1, it is simply a reissue of the Hawk F4U-1D reviewed beginning on page 73 of The F4U Corsair in Detail & Scale, Part 1. Hawk made no changes to the kit to represent the many differences between the F4U-1D and the AU-1. Even as an F4U-1D, the kit is very poor and cannot be recommended.

Italeri F4U-5N

While this kit does have a number of problems and inaccuracies, it is clearly the best 1/72nd scale model available of any of the later Corsair variants.

Surface detailing is in the form of engraved panel lines which are generally well executed except for the cowl flaps which are too deep and heavy. The representation of the circular access panels in the top of the left horizontal stabilizer and the bottom of the right stabilizer are scribed into the plastic. These were on Corsairs up through the F4U-4/-4B, but they were not on the "dash 5" variants. The formation lights under each wing are missing and should be added by scribing them in place and painting them blue.

While he was in the Navy, Walt Fink served with Guy Bordelon, who was the Navy's only ace during the Korean War. Walt built Italeri's 1/72nd scale F4U-5N and marked it to represent Bordelon's famous night fighting Corsair from VC-3. **(Fink)**

The fuselage has the correct exhausts, and the extensions are separate parts. The mounting locations for the exhaust glare shields are molded as small lines, and the shields are separate pieces to be glued in place. The cowl flaps are the correct shape and size, and the proper number of flaps is represented. But the forward fuselage is too short for the F4U-5N. This can be corrected by inserting plugs made from stock sheet plastic just aft of the cowl flaps. The drawings in this book can be used to ascertain the correct length.

The wings are set up to be used for several different versions. Flashed-over holes are available for various pylon combinations. For the F4U-5N, the stub pylons are provided, but there are no rockets to go on them. A single external fuel tank is included to go on the centerline station, however these were usually carried on one of the pylons under the center wing section. The kit provides no center wing pylons or stores. The cannon barrels are separate parts, and they are well executed with the appropriate flash suppressors on them. The gun bay detail is nicely scribed, but the shell ejector chutes are simply recessed marks that need to be opened up.

The engine is a one-piece unit with the forward row of cylinders molded to a firewall. There is no representation of the aft row of cylinders. The crankcase is too rounded, and more closely represents the one used on earlier Corsairs rather than on the R-2800-32W engine. It should be more cylindrical and have dozens of bolts covering its surface. It might be possible to find a correct after-market engine or use one from another kit.

The cockpit has a floor, consoles, seat, instrument panel, and control column. But the instrument panel is incorrect, having the center panel between the rudder pedals. This was on the F4U-4/-4B, but not on the F4U-5 series of Corsairs. Simply cut this center panel off in the appropriate place. The panel and the consoles have nice raised features that are easy to paint.

The windscreen and canopy are separate clear parts that are a little thick. The forward two frames on the windscreen are noticeably too far apart. The canopy can be displayed opened or closed, but it does not really capture the blown appearance of the real thing.

The main gear wells are enclosed and molded into the underside of the wings. Detailing is present, but the wells are too shallow. There is no detailing in the tail gear well.

The struts are fairly accurate, but they are slightly too thick below the oleos. The oleo scissors are too thick, but they can be thinned down with a razor knife. Ejection pin marks need to be removed from the upper main struts. The retraction arms are provided as separate pieces, and they are the best available in any 1/72nd scale kit of the Corsair. The main gear doors for each side are molded as one piece, and they must be carefully cut apart. The detailing on both sides is quite good. The forward main gear doors and both tail wheel doors also have good details on both sides. The main wheels are each two pieces, and they look accurate and in scale. The tail gear is well represented and has retraction arms that are provided as a separate "U"-shaped part.

Two pieces are glued together to make the radome for the right wing, but there is no indication as to exactly where it is to be positioned. Follow the drawings in this book to insure that it is located properly. Fit is not good, and some filling and sanding around it will be required.

Although there are several problems with this model, none are very difficult to fix. The main effort must be directed at correcting the fuselage length. If this is done, a very nice replica of an F4U-5N can be built.

Jim Roeder and J. C. Bahr contributed to this review.

Italeri F4U-7 & AU-1

This kit is basically the same as the one for the F4U-5N reviewed above, but there are a number of options and extra parts provided. The box art on the front states that the model is an F4U-7, but the artwork on the back shows an AU-1. Basically, the kit can be used to build either of these versions as well as the F4U-5 and F4U-5N.

The points covered in the review immediately above apply to this model as well. Comments here will be limited to the extra and optional parts included in this issue.

Cowl rings for the F4U-5/-5N, F4U-7, and AU-1 are all included. If the one for the F4U-7 is used, a fairing is provided to achieve the proper shape. The fuselage is the correct length for the F4U-7, but not the AU-1 or F4U-5. The engine detail is different from the F4U-5N kit covered above, however, only the fronts of the rear cylinders are depicted. The crankcase is devoid of any details, but the propeller is quite accurate in shape and detail.

This French Corsair was built by J. C. Bahr, who used the Italeri 1/72nd scale F4U-7/AU-1 kit. (Liles)

Ten five-inch rockets are included to go on the wing pylons which are supplied in this issue, and two fuel tanks are provided for the pylons under the center wing section. Four cannon barrels, with their appropriate fairings, are included as separate pieces, but the barrels project from the rounded front of the fairing instead of being recessed as they should be. It is necessary to remove them, drill out the fairings slightly, and reglue the barrels in the correct location.

Overall, we like this kit better than the F4U-5N issue covered above. Having the two pylons that go under the center wing section is a nice plus as are the two external fuel tanks. The F4U-5N, as well as the other versions, can be built from this one kit because of the optional parts that are provided.

Jim Roeder and J. C. Bahr contributed to this review.

Matchbox F4U-4

The box art says the kit is an F4U-4, but the model comes with the 20-mm cannon of an F4U-4B. These are separate parts which do not have to be used, and this makes it easy to build an F4U-4 instead. We actually recommend doing this, because the scribing for the gun bay panels, as well as the shell chutes under the wings, are correct for the F4U-4 with its six .50-caliber machine guns. To use the cannon, much of this needs to be re-worked, especially the shell chutes.

Typical of so many Matchbox kits, this model has very deeply scribed surface detail that detracts from the appearance of the model. Some features are left off, while others are not accurately represented. For example the step in the inboard right flap is indicated only by a scribed line rather than a hole in the flap. A similar step is also scribed in the inboard left flap, and it should not be there at all. Small access panels are indicated by recessed circular holes that need to be filled in and sanded out. The access panels on the horizontal stabilizers are represented by scribed circles as they should be, but they are on the tops of both stabilizers. They should be on the top of the left and bottom of the right stabilizer.

The propeller is the correct diameter, but the blades are too thin. The engine is inaccurate and lacking in detail. We took an engine from a Hasegawa kit, modified the crankcase to look like the one on an R-2800-18W, and used it inside the cowling. The scoop under the cowl ring is too flat, and it must be reworked to get the correct shape.

No cockpit detail is included except for a pilot figure and a crude seat. After replacing the cockpit details in a Hasegawa F4U-1 with a True Details interior to achieve the correct floorless cockpit of a "dash one" Corsair, we had the cockpit parts from the Hasegawa kit left over. These worked nicely as a basis for building an interior for this Matchbox model. The canopy and windscreen are molded as one piece, and they represent the earlier style rounded windscreen used on the F4U-4. It would be difficult to replace it with the flat windscreen used on most F4U-4s.

The landing gear wells are open and completely devoid of detailing. The struts are very thin, except for the oleo scissors which are too large. Retraction arms on the main struts are incomplete and inaccurate. The main

The only F4U-4 presently available in 1/72nd scale is the rather poor Matchbox kit. This one was built by Nick Waters, who chose Honduran markings for his model.

wheels are crude and should be replaced with a set from True Details. The gear doors have no detailing on the inner surfaces.

While this model has some significant shortcomings, it is clearly better than the Fujimi F4U-4/-4B, and it is the only kit presently available of this version of the Corsair. Any modeler who wants to add a 1/72nd scale F4U-4 or -4B to his collection must start with this kit, but he should be prepared to spend a lot of time correcting the inaccuracies and adding the details to this model.

1/48th SCALE KITS

Academy/Minicraft F4U-4

We rate this as the best 1/48th scale F4U-4 that has been released to date. Surface detailing is excellent and features recessed panel lines and very nice fabric areas. Our only complaint here is that the boarding step in the inboard right flap is missing, so it must be opened up by the modeler.

Engine detailing is pretty good, except that the crankcase is too rounded and narrow at the front. The photographs on page 35 illustrate what the crankcase should look like. The cylinders are molded on the firewall, and while it would have been better to have separate rows of cylinders, these will be adequate for most modelers once the assembly is installed inside the cowling. The propeller is accurate, and the hub has correct detailing.

The cockpit consists of an instrument panel, stick, seat, rear bulkhead, and a floor with the two side consoles. The seat is the conventional design instead of the correct bucket and flat armor plate configuration used in the F4U-4. It should be replaced with one that is more accurate. Otherwise, the cockpit is adequate, but the True Details resin cockpit for this kit, and the F4U-4B covered below, is significantly better and worth the effort and expense. It is True Details item 48452. The windscreen and canopy are separate parts that may be assembled opened or closed. The windscreen is the later flat design, but the two forward frames are too far apart and are almost parallel. They should be closer together, and the width between them decreases from bottom to top. (See the photographs on page 13 and the scale drawings for the correct alignment of these frames.) This is a

problem found on most models of the later Corsair variants that had the flat windscreen.

The holes for the guns and the shell chutes must be opened up by the modeler. The kit was engineered this way so that it could also be issued as an F4U-4B. The two pylons under the center wing section are molded as part of the lower wing half, and two 150-gallon fuel tanks are included as stores.

The landing gear wells are enclosed, but the forward portion of the main wells is too shallow. The aft main gear doors have detailing on the inside, but the forward doors do not. Likewise, the tail gear doors, as well as the tail wheel well, is devoid of any detailing. The main gear struts have ejector pin marks, and the oleo scissors are too thick. It would be best to thin these down or replace them with ones made form plastic strips. The retraction struts are slightly too short, so they do not quite touch the interior of the wheel well. The main wheels are well executed with accurate brake and spoke detailing, and the tires have a nice diamond tread.

As mentioned earlier, the fabric areas are well represented with vapor honing, but the very top of the horizontal stabilizer on the left side was also honed by mistake. This should be sanded and polished smooth. Check the right side of the tail to see the area where the honing should be removed.

With very little work, this kit can be completed as an excellent model. It can be enhanced by adding rockets under the wings, but these must be obtained from another kit.

Academy Minicraft F4U-4B

This is basically the same as the F4U-4 kit covered above, and of the two, it is the only one presently available. A separate tree of parts is included that provides the 20-mm cannon, stub pylons, eight 5-inch rockets, and two 500-pound bombs. These weapons are a welcome addition to what is provided in the F4U-4 model.

To build the F4U-4B, the instructions indicate which shell chutes and holes should be opened up for the four cannon in the leading edge of the wing. Otherwise, the model is exactly the same as the F4U-4 covered above.

When building an F4U-4B, we recommend this kit

At present, the Academy/Minicraft kits are the best F4U-4 and F4U-4B models in 1/48th scale. Jim Roeder built the F4U-4B issue in the markings of VF-53. (Roeder)

over the Hasegawa model, because the rockets, pylons, and cannon in this kit are nicely molded plastic parts rather than the white metal parts provided by Hasegawa.

Jim Roeder contributed to the reviews of the Academy/Minicraft kits.

Hasegawa F4U-4

Hasegawa's F4U-4 is very similar to the one from Academy/Minicraft, but it has raised panel lines instead of the recessed detailing found on the Academy/Minicraft issue. For this reason, we give a slight edge to the Academy/Minicraft F4U-4 as being the better choice to build. In almost every other respect, the two models are practically identical. The step in the right inboard flap is present on this model, however, and it will save the modeler the time and effort needed to cut it out on the Academy/Minicraft model.

The design of the engine parts are essentially the same, and like the Academy/Minicraft kit, the crankcase is too narrow and rounded on this model as well.

The cockpit design and layout is also similar to that in the Academy/Minicraft model, and here again, the incorrect seat design is provided. Verlinden's detail set will prove helpful, and although it is expensive, it does include other parts like dropped wing flaps and etched metal cowl flaps. The windscreen and canopy are separate parts that can be assembled opened or closed. The windscreen is the later flat design, but the forward two frames are too far apart and are angled incorrectly. This is the same problem found in the Academy/Minicraft kits.

The two pylons under the center wing section are molded as part of the lower wing, and two 150-gallon fuel tanks are included to go on them. But there are no bombs provided as options, nor are there any rockets or launch stubs for the outer wing panels.

The main gear wells are enclosed and have some detailing. The forward area is a bit deeper than on the Academy/Minicraft model, but it is still too shallow. The

Dave Pluth used the Hasegawa 1/48th scale F4U-4 to build this model of a Corsair from VF-193. These are the markings that come in the kit. The main difference between the Hasegawa and Academy/Minicraft F4U-4 kits in 1/48th scale is that the Hasegawa model has raised panel lines, while the Academy/Minicraft kit has recessed lines. **(Pluth)**

tail wheel well is also too shallow and lacks detailing. The struts have mold pin marks, and again, the oleo scissors should be thinned a little. The retraction arms are separate pieces, and as with the Academy/Minicraft kits, they are slightly too short and do not quite reach the top of the wheel well. The main gear wheels are nicely detailed, and the tires have a diamond tread. However, there are two pin marks on the inside of each tire that need to be removed.

Except for the fact that this model has raised panel lines, it is practically the same as the Academy/Minicraft F4U-4. Both can be used to build excellent models if care is taken to correct a few inaccuracies.

Hasegawa F4U-4B

This model is exactly the same as the Hasegawa F4U-4 covered immediately above. Hasegawa simply included white metal parts for the 20-mm cannon and stub pylons. These metal parts do not fit well, and have to be primed and sanded before painting. The modeler needs to open up the outer two shell ejector slots under the wings and fill in the indention for the inner one. Hasegawa also included two trees from their 1/48th scale P-51D kit that provide 5-inch rockets and two 500-pound bombs.

In selecting a 1/48th scale F4U-4B, we recommend the Academy/Minicraft kit over this one, because the plastic parts fit better and are easier to work with.

Jim Roeder contributed to the Hasegawa reviews.

Hasegawa's 1/48th scale F4U-4B was used by Jim Roeder to build this Corsair in the markings of VMF-332.
(Roeder)

Heller F4U-7

The F4U-7 was produced exclusively for the French Navy, so it is not hard to understand why the only 1/48th scale kit of the F4U-7 is from the French model company, Heller. Surface detailing is in the form of raised panel lines which are generally accurate. But the plastic is rather soft, so be extra careful not to remove any lines when sanding. The shell ejector chutes under the wings are indented, so they should be opened up to provide a more realistic appearance.

The shape and size of the propeller is fine, but the hub lacks detailing. Although both rows of cylinders are represented, many details are not included on the engine. The crankcase is too rounded and lacks the very noticeable bolts. These problems are particularly conspicuous on such a large model.

The same thing can be said about the cockpit interior. There are several parts, but the detailing and accuracy need improving. No details are molded into the instrument panel or side consoles. By using some scrap plastic and other small parts, the appearance of the cockpit can be improved considerably. The ProModeler decal sheet 88-1021 has instrument panels and seat belts for Corsairs. Although none of the panels are specifically for the F4U-7, individual instruments are included, and these will look much more realistic than the instrument panel decal provided in the kit. The windscreen and canopy are separate parts that can be assembled in the opened or closed position. The forward braces on the windscreen are a little too far apart, but they are better than on the Academy/Minicraft and Hasegawa models.

Perhaps the strong point of the kit is the main landing gear. It consists of several parts that fit together well, and it looks realistic and in scale when completed. The wells are enclosed, and the interior of the doors have appropriate detailing. Detailing on the main wheels is good, and the tires have a diamond tread. The tail wheel assembly is incorrect, because it is too short. It needs to be lengthened to the taller design used on all Corsairs beginning with the F4U-1A. The tail gear doors are molded on the sides of the fuselage, and there is no representation of the tail gear well at all.

Ten pylons are included for the outer wing panels, and there are ten rockets to mount on them. The warheads of the rockets look very unusual, but they could represent some used by the French that we are unfamiliar with. Although U. S. 5-inch rockets were sometimes fitted with warheads which were larger in diameter than the rockets themselves, they did not look like what is represented in this kit. The two pylons that go under the center wing section are also provided, and there are fuel tanks to go on them. The centerline pylon, used on F4U-5s, AU-1s, and F4U-7s, is included, but there is no store for it. See page 73 for a photograph of this pylon.

Although we usually restrict our comments to an objective review of each kit's features, we do make statements about fit when specific problems do exist that require extra attention. The fit of this kit is poor throughout. The large pins that are supposed to line up the fuselage are more of a problem than a help, and it is easier to remove most or all of them before joining the parts. Cut off the tops of both pins on the tail gear and glue it in place at the end of assembly. The fit of the cowl is poor, and the wings are not much better. Again cut off the two locator pins at the back of the wing near the fuselage, because they do not line up correctly. Once you have the parts together, be ready to do a lot of filling and sanding.

Heller AU-1

This kit is essentially the same as the F4U-7 release covered immediately above. It has a different front cowl ring without the lower scoop, and the rockets have been deleted. Two 500-pound bombs are included for the two center wing pylons. The two 150-gallon fuel tanks also remain as options, but there are no stores for the ten

The only AU-1 available in 1/48th scale is this model from Heller, but it does not have the correct fuselage length or cowl shape for an AU-1. Stan Parker chose the well known markings of VMA-212's "Lancers" to complete his model. (Parker)

smaller pylons that fit under the outer wing sections.

When Heller engineered this kit, they molded the forward fuselage as two separate pieces, and the cowl ring was also separate. It would appear that this was done so that the different forward fuselage sections of the late Corsair variants could be included as necessary. So it is hard to understand why the longer forward fuselage with its bulged fairings is not included in this kit. Likewise, the AU-1 also had the bulges in the cowl ring where the cheek scoops were on the F4U-5, although the scoops themselves were not present on the AU-1. But the cowl ring is perfectly circular in this kit rather than having the bulges on either side. In short, the kit does not have an accurate forward fuselage for an AU-1.

Stan Parker contributed to this review.

Lindberg F4U-5N

One of the oldest Corsair kits in 1/48th scale, this Lindberg model is very crude and inaccurate by today's standards. It does not even have wells for the landing gear. To their credit, Lindberg did get the length of the forward fuselage right, but otherwise the kit is so inaccurate that it cannot be used as the basis for an authentic scale model. The kit was issued several times by Lindberg, and it has also been released by Testors in a three-pack with a P-51D Mustang and P-47D Thunderbolt.

Minicraft F4U-5 & F4U-5N

Released just as this book was being published, this kit can be built as an F4U-5 or F4U-5N. However, the decals only provide markings for Guy Bordelon's F4U-5N. Except for the old Lindberg kit, this is the only 1/48th scale Corsair model to have the correct longer fuselage appropriate to the F4U-5 variants and the AU-1. But unfortunately, as the forward fuselage was lengthened, the wing was also moved forward. As a result, the leading edge of the wing is too close to the exhausts and aft edge of the cowl flaps. It would take some careful plastic surgery, but it would not be too difficult to move the wing aft about 3/16ths of an inch. This would involve

Minicraft's F4U-5/-5N is the best kit to use when building a 1/48th scale model of a "dash 5" Corsair. (Minicraft)

cutting away some plastic on the underside of the fuselage assembly where the aft end of the wing assembly joins it. Some filling would then be required to close the gap at the forward end of the wing assembly where it meets the underside of the fuselage.

The engine has two complete rows of cylinders, but the crankcase is the rounded bullet design used on the earlier versions of the R-2800 engine. It should be the cylindrical design with the large bolts as illustrated on page 35. This problem presently exists with all 1/48th scale models of the F4U-4 and later Corsair variants. We know of no after-market R-2800 engines with the correct crankcase design. The only 1/48th scale kit we know of that has the correct crankcase is the ProModeler P-47N Thunderbolt. The modeler must choose between cannibalizing a ProModeler P-47N or scratchbuilding a correct crankcase for the engine as it comes in this Corsair kit.

The cockpit has a floor with the two side consoles molded into it. The instrument panel correctly does not have the center console between the rudder pedals, and the details are provided by decals. Appropriate instrument panels for both the F4U-5 and F4U-5N are included, and the one for the night fighter has the radar scope at the center. The seat is correct for the later versions of the Corsair. The bucket is a separate part, and the vertical armor back is molded as part of the aft bulkhead. Some modelers will want to add some raised detailing to the panels and consoles, particularly if the canopy is displayed in the opened position.

The windscreen and canopy are molded in two parts, and may be assembled opened or closed. As with most other kits of the later Corsair variants, the forward frames on the windscreen are too far apart and are almost parallel. Instead, they should angle toward each other from bottom to top.

The wing is correct for the F4U-5 in that it has the 20-mm cannon with their appropriate shell ejector slots, the staggered pylons, and correct representation of the gun bay panels in the recessed scribing. Further, the fabric panels have been replaced with metal panels on the outer wing sections. Only the left aileron should have a trim tab, but one is scribed into the right aileron as well.

The landing gear is very much like that found in the Academy/Minicraft F4U-4 and F4U-4B kits covered above, but the main wheels are quite different. Each is two pieces, and they have open spokes and weighted tires. The open spokes do not look right, and the tire is too

weighted for a carrier-based aircraft. We recommend replacing these with the True Details wheels and tires for the F4U and F6F. This is True Details item 48045.

Two 1,000-pound bombs, two 150-gallon fuel tanks, and eight 5-inch rockets are provided as external stores. The flash shields above the exhausts are too symmetrical in shape, but they can be easily corrected, or new ones can be made from plastic card. The retractable boarding step is not represented in the surface detail, and the blue formation lights under the wing tips are a bit too far forward. All of this is relatively minor and simple to correct.

Except for the fact that the wing is located too far forward, this is a pretty good kit, and it has the longer fuselage found on the F4U-5s and the AU-1. If the crankcase is corrected, the wing is moved aft, and a few fairly simple problems are remedied, a very nice model of the F4U-5 or F4U-5N can be produced. We also recommend using this model to build a 1/48th scale AU-1. By filling in the cheek scoops and sanding them down a bit, and by adding the pylons and a few other parts from the Heller AU-1, a much more accurate AU-1 can be built from this kit than can be from the Heller model.

Monogram F4U-4B

Although it is not as old as the Lindberg model, this kit dates back to 1963 and has some of the toy-like features found on models from that era. As is always the case, these features detract from the accuracy of the finished model. The wheels roll, the landing gear retracts, the wings fold, the arresting hook operates up and down, and the propeller spins.

There is no detailing in the cockpit except for a rear bulkhead, pilot, and a crude instrument panel that is covered by a decal. The early style rounded windscreen and canopy are clear pieces. Most of the framework is molded as part of the fuselage halves, and this results in a very poor fit. The engine is molded into the front of the cowling, and the gear wells are devoid of any detail.

Rockets are included to go under the wings, but they are on launch stubs like those found on the F4U-4 instead of the F4U-4B which the kit represents. A radome is also provided, but only one F4U-4N was produced.

In short, this kit is best left to the collectors and nostalgia buffs. The Academy/Minicraft and Hasegawa F4U-4 and F4U-4B models are much better choices when it comes to selecting a 1/48th scale kit to build.

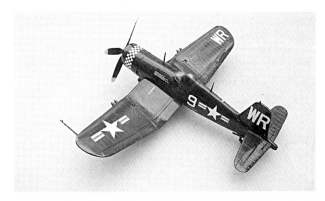

Bob Bartolacci used the old Monogram F4U-4B to build this model of a Corsair from VMA-312. This older model is not up to the standards found in the Minicraft and Hasegawa kits. (Bartolacci)

More Detail and Scale Titles from squadron/signal publications....

8250 P-51 Mustang Part 1

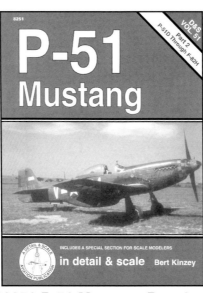

8251 P-51 Mustang Part 2

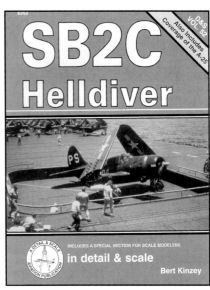

8252 SB2C Helldiver

8253 TBF & TBM Avenger

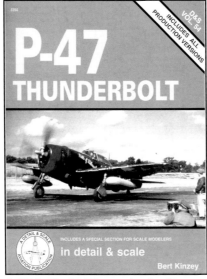

8254 P-47 Thunderbolt

8255 F4U Corsair